*journeys to the nearby*

# JOURNEYS
## TO THE NEARBY

*a gardener discovers
the gentle art of untravelling*

## ELSPETH BRADBURY

RONSDALE PRESS

JOURNEYS TO THE NEARBY
Copyright © 2025 Elspeth Bradbury

All rights reserved, including those for text and data mining, A.I. training, and similar technologies. No part of this publication may be reproduced, stored in a retrieval system, or transmitted, in any form or by any means, without prior written permission of the publisher, or, in Canada, in the case of photocopying or other reprographic copying, a licence from Access Copyright (the Canadian Copyright Licensing Agency).

All illustrations by Elspeth Bradbury except "Tarxacum officinale" by Erwin Lichtenegger on page 160 (reprinted with permission of Monika Sobotik) and "Animalcules as observed by Anton van Leeuwenhoek" c.1795 on page 229.

RONSDALE PRESS
125A – 1030 Denman Street, Vancouver, BC Canada V6G 2M6
www.ronsdalepress.com

Book Design: John van der Woude, JVDW Designs
Cover Design: Jean Bradbury
Editor: Pearl Luke
Copy Editor: Kevin Welsh

Ronsdale Press wishes to thank the following for their support of its publishing program: the Canada Council for the Arts, the Government of Canada, the British Columbia Arts Council, and the Province of British Columbia through the British Columbia Book Publishing Tax Credit program.

Library and Archives Canada Cataloguing in Publication
Title: Journeys to the nearby : a gardener discovers the gentle art of untravelling / Elspeth Bradbury.
Names: Bradbury, Elspeth, 1939- author
Identifiers: Canadiana (print) 20240483847 | Canadiana (ebook) 20240483383 | ISBN 9781553807247 (softcover) | ISBN 9781553807254 (EPUB)
Subjects: LCSH: Bradbury, Elspeth, 1939- | LCSH: Gardening—Humor. | LCSH: Backyard gardens—Humor.
Classification: LCC SB450.97 .B73 2025 | DDC 635—dc23

At Ronsdale Press we are committed to protecting the environment. To this end we are working with Canopy and printers to phase out our use of paper produced from ancient forests. This book is one step towards that goal.

Printed in Canada

*For family and friends who've been there for me every step of the way.*

# An Invitation

The winter holiday came and went, and I'm still on a reading binge, gorging on travel writers as if they were chocolate truffles. I baked shortbread while legendary English traveller Bruce Chatwin introduced me to a cast of seriously unsettling Patagonians. I finished off the eggnog while American writer Paul Theroux sweltered doggedly through another African safari. I made — and promptly broke — a resolution to walk every day around the block while Canadian adventurer Bruce Kirkby embraced the vast and untamed wilderness. Such nerve! Such dash! Such disasters! Their exploits left me gripping the arms of my recliner, heartily glad I was snug at home with a cup of herbal tea before bedtime.

The more travel books I consume, the more I wonder why these writers embark on such gruelling journeys in the first place. Why do they weary themselves half to death, put up with suffocating heat, perishing cold, mosquitoes and the dreaded runs? I don't have to look far for answers. Curiosity, they explain: to put off living or to make a living, to claim bragging rights, to escape from responsibilities, from creditors, from the rat race, from relationships gone sour. Bruce Kirkby flees from boredom and a stifling office cubicle. Paul Theroux comments, "Of course, it's much harder to stay home and be polite to people and face things." Bruce Chatwin, trying to account for his insane restlessness and pondering penguin migrations, wonders if we also have journeys mapped out in our central nervous systems.

I enjoy the tales of travellers who set their sights on physical rather than cultural landscapes. These writers often make a point of explaining that their exploits bring them closer to nature. Heaven knows I'm all for that, but I can't help feeling they'd rather pit themselves against the natural world than embrace it. Titles such as *The Fearful Void* or *Alone Against the North* are telling. Does it have to be so hard to experience nature intimately? Not at all, they tell me airily, it's nearby. To prove the point, British writer Robert Macfarlane saunters through his local woodland in a windstorm, climbs a tree and describes the experience with his usual pinpoint accuracy. Great stuff! But a swaying beech tree evidently doesn't cut it, and before you can say vamoose, he's off again to cling to a distant precipice or squirm down a faraway hole in the ground. American Barry Lopez, another traveller who focuses on nature, also chooses stormy weather for his contemplative camping trip to appropriately named Cape Foulweather in his home state of Oregon, then he too is up and away to go about as far as anyone can go, at least on this planet. Coincidentally, both writers quote William Blake's understandably overworked advice, "To see a world in a grain of sand / and a heaven in a wild flower," although sand for these obsessive travellers morphs quickly into something a whole lot bigger.

I too want to see the world, but here I am stuck like a schlump in this recliner with a lapful of admirably up-and-at-it, on-the-move writers. What's to be done about it? I'd rather sleep on a bed of nails than rack up my carbon footprint, crammed into the centre seat of a long-haul aircraft. Mulling things over, I've decided that perhaps I don't have to check the expiry date on my passport just yet. From my own meagre experience, the best reason for any of us to pack our bags is for the heightened awareness that new surroundings induce in us. Travel documentaries open up the world wonderfully, but however skillful the cinematography, they can only go so far. When we set foot on unfamiliar ground, all our senses shift into high gear. Our observations grow more acute, and we make memories. We feel alive. Uncomfortable possibly, miserable maybe, but alive. Wouldn't it be possible to feel that kind of intensity and sleep in our own beds at the same time?

I'm hatching a plan.

I shall set out on a journey of my own. In reality, a series of small journeys. I won't, however, be tangling with airport security or slogging it out in the back of beyond. My destination will lie no farther than our own backyard.

We are fortunate, my husband Ray and I, to have the run of a woodsy patch of suburbia that slopes down from front to back, shaded by a forested park across a narrow road. We've gardened it for more than thirty years, walked over it, grubbed about in it, loved and cursed it. Every inch is familiar, so how can I approach it with new eyes and the anticipation of impending adventure? I'll simply walk outside and wait. Take one step and then another, take my time, look and listen, touch and sniff, try to satisfy my curiosity, make some drawings and — this is important — I'll think like a travel writer and send back reports.

Join me on my journeys, and I promise we won't end up exhausted, blistered, frostbitten or diseased. The world we'll travel lies a comfortable halfway between the globe and William Blake's grain of sand. If we're lucky, we'll make a few discoveries, stumble upon a few surprises, and if we're very lucky, we may even catch a glimpse of that heaven in a wildflower.

# The Journey Begins

*S*hortbread and eggnog are already distant memories. The new year is underway, and I'm growing restless. It's late afternoon, and the rain has finally tailed off to drizzle. A typical January day in Vancouver. I feel a little tense, as one does, embarking on a journey. I stuff myself into a padded jacket, decide against a hat, open the door, sniff the air, return for the hat and start.

Three paces forward and turn left...

...step down from the deck...

...three more paces to the left.

Behind me, the living room windows glow softly, invitingly. In front of me, the ground slopes away in a dusky haze. The heavy fronds of a large cedar hang low overhead and drip steadily onto the gravel path and the shady bed below. Although this bed is planted with several old azaleas, they are leafless now, and I can scarcely pick out their skimpy forms in the half-light. Underneath them, the bleached stalks of last summer's daylilies tilt among the ragged stems of phlox and the splayed fronds of hellebores. I stare at this bedraggled scene for several minutes. The earth doesn't move and neither do I. Five minutes into my project and I'm faltering?

*Take your time!* I wipe a dribble of rain from my face and concentrate on the hellebores. They may be flattened, but their dark green foliage almost hides the clammy soil and glistens in a healthy waterproof way. *Look closely.* Each leaf is made up of leaflets joined at the centre. They are perfectly familiar to me, yet I have no idea how many leaflets make up the whole. I count them. Six . . . five . . . nine. How strange. Some spring from the centre and some split into two or three parts. As discoveries go, this doesn't rank with penicillin, but it's a small find for me and that's encouraging. I'm not on the lookout, after all, for high adventure in the Hindu Kush.

I leave, letting the hard-working hellebores harvest whatever sustenance they can from the thin winter light, move farther along the shady path, and stand for another few minutes hoping that something more riveting will show up. It doesn't. Obviously, I was far too optimistic in assuming that the garden would deliver fascinating observations at a moment's notice. It's getting chilly out here, so I'll wait a couple more minutes, then pack it in.

I'm already retracing my steps when something makes me hesitate. A movement? A sound? It takes a moment to identify "something" as a faint waft of deliciousness. Flowers? In January? I'd forgotten, as I do every year, that sweet box grows here at the back of the shady bed. This humble shrub with its spidery white blooms is easy to ignore until suddenly, at this neediest time of year, it offers up a gift of ethereal fragrance, a scent that exists beyond the reach of words. I can only describe it as a taste, a draft of thirst-quenching, soul-refreshing nectar. June's lilies and roses, glorious as they are, never arouse in me this kind of poignant emotion that brings me to the brink of tears. The drizzle is returning, but I stand heedless, marvelling.

# A Visitor

A fter a shaky start, the fragrant finale of my first expedition has spurred me on to add more steps to my journey. I walk briskly to the end of the shady path, where two black compost bins stand under an old apple tree. They are lidded and cylindrical, not exactly eye candy, but they do hold our green waste and turn it into organic soil for the veggie patch, which runs alongside the neighbour's fence below. I planned to expound at length on the joys of composting, but instead, I'm smiling ruefully, remembering an incident that came to be known as "The Great Bear Shindig."

A third bin used to stand in front of these two. One night in the fall a few years ago, I woke to persistent thumping and the crashing of car doors, and I reckoned sleepily that our normally quiet neighbours were enjoying an enviably lively get-together. The following morning, we discovered the uproar had indeed been down to neighbours. Sort of. Bears have visited our garden in the past, and certainly more often than we know because, every year, they find their way down from the mountains to forage among the lush coastal vegetation. The local parks department dutifully erects CAUTION BEAR IN AREA signs in the park across the road, which everyone ignores except for tourists from bear-deficient countries who are understandably concerned about being eaten.

The visiting bears had never been a problem until the night of the compost robbery. We stared in awe at the aftermath. The bin itself was reduced to plastic shards, some dangling in the shady bed, some tossed across the fence into the neighbours' lot. The lid had been chucked as lightly as a Frisbee across the leeks and kale. A team of lumberjacks armed with sledgehammers couldn't have done a better demolition job. Remnants of the compost remained in a slumping heap, but most were strewn about the path: squishy black banana skins, smashed eggshells, rotting cabbage leaves, torn tea bags and gobs of matter too far gone to be named, all well mashed into the gravel. And I had only myself to blame.

From time to time, the apple tree, which spreads its gnarly branches over the bins, sometimes surprises us with a usable crop. Last year, however, its meagre, scabby offering barely warranted picking, let alone turning into applesauce. I'm bear aware enough to know that leaving the ground littered with overripe windfalls is asking for trouble, so I'd tossed them into the front bin and fastened down the lid. Sense of smell is vitally important to these animals, so what was I thinking? That a thin sheet of plastic could come between a trove of fragrantly decomposing apples and a twitching bear nose? Some hefty shoves, a few well-aimed swipes, a hug or two, and the bin must have cracked like a nut.

Much smacking of lips would have followed before the robber was off down the road to sniff out the next irresistible odour and another obliging human. No shortage of us around.

Terry, a neighbour and bird lover, kept a feeder topped up with seeds for the chickadees. She hung it from the top of a steel pole as tall as a lamp standard, which made it squirrel-proof but not, as it turned out, bear-proof. The empty feeder, only slightly bashed, turned up a few days later, but the hefty pole never did straighten out. Another friend packed her hard-earned blackberry pickings into a spare chest freezer but left the sliding door to her basement unlatched. Even the plastic freezer bags disappeared. Such incidents are a nuisance for us, but in the end, they are usually much worse for the bears which, once accustomed to human provisions, are considered dangerous and must often be relocated or killed.

Feeling a little chastened, I turn and plod back along the shady path, which is growing rapidly shadier as the short winter day slips away. So ends my second journey. Have I managed to experience the world more vividly? Has it surprised me? Well, I certainly hadn't expected to remember the infamous shindig, so perhaps that counts for something.

# The Boss

*Four paces to the right.*

I'm standing on the deck where a red hummingbird feeder hangs directly outside the kitchen window. In front of me, the window box is filled with evergreens and sprigs of holly. This Christmassy arrangement is looking shabby, and I'm contemplating its removal when a sudden whirr warns me of an incoming bird. I freeze. He hovers indecisively, decides I'm harmless and perches to feed only inches from my face.

I usually see these Anna's hummingbirds from inside the house, where they appear as dark silhouettes. Lit by the low sun behind my shoulder, this bird flares into brilliant, iridescent colour. His slim back is shingled with tiny emerald feathers, and his ruby-red bib is pulled up over his head like a balaclava.

It's tempting to describe hummingbirds as flying jewels, but lumps of rock don't fizz with life. This bird's entire body quivers with pent-up energy, and as he drinks, his long threadlike tongue flickers in and out at lightning speed. I have a sudden urge to reach out and cup this pulsing creature in my hands. What an odd reaction! Is it a protective instinct, to calm his incessant edginess, or is it a relentless human desire for ownership or for some kind of relationship with other living creatures? Of course, the thought of picking a hummingbird off a feeder is beyond ludicrous. He doesn't let his guard down for an instant and could take off like a rocket.

Still standing inches from the feeder, I shift my weight, and the bird throws me a wary glance. He is almost certainly Alf, the neighbourhood's alpha male, who considers it his duty to exercise exclusive rights over this handy source of nectar. From his favourite perch in the nearby star magnolia, he launches ferocious attacks on interlopers, who usually take off in a hurry. Only occasionally does a rival dare to make a stand and engage in a vertical skirmish, a brief battle of wills before the boss, flashing boastful colours, returns to his twig in triumph.

This tiny tyrant seems in no hurry to leave. He sips, glances at me, sips again. For the last year, he's been growing accustomed to my presence as I refill the feeders or simply go about my business.

Today, this small shining creature has granted me a rare intimacy. I don't even have time to duck as he lifts off with another whirr, swoops across the garden and disappears into the 'Yuletide' camellia. For all I know, he's perched there now in full view. All winter long, this generous shrub produces blooms of the same red as Alf's bib, and the disguise fails only when Alf flashes his warning lights — blinks of screaming scarlet that no flower could achieve.

# Snow Day

When we went to bed last night, the garden was already tucked under a thin white eiderdown. This morning, the circular table on the deck has turned into a giant snow cake, and the chairs around it are piled with enormous puffy cushions. There hasn't been a breath of wind overnight, so every bare twig carries a precariously balanced load, every post wears a tottering gnome cap, and every evergreen branch bows down beneath a heavy burden.

Snowfalls around here usually amount to little more than pretty atmospheric effects that melt away in hours, but occasionally, winter does it in style. Dire warnings flood the local media, hardware stores run out of salt or shovels, and families rediscover sleds while the rest of Canada smirks politely.

Although the world appears newly magical, there will be no loitering on my journey today, no idling to admire the transformation. The snow weighing down the evergreens is beautiful but damaging, and there's urgent work to do. All the same, I pause at the door to take my first breaths of cold air and watch the big soft flakes waltz down. An eerie silence has fallen on the garden. We live in a quiet area, but this is an altogether different quiet — a complete lull in the normal daily hum. Not a single car braves our unploughed roadway.

Ray, well prepared as usual, has propped a shovel and a rake under the eaves by the door. I hold the rake upside-down and use the handle to probe while I shuffle across the deck and down the steps. I'm wearing mittens, a down coat over a thick sweater and a knitted hat pulled well down over my ears. If Alf is watching, he won't recognize the lumpy creature invading his territory. We have plenty of food in the house and no urgent need to drive anywhere, so we may not bother clearing a path through the white desert, that used to be our driveway, to the giant mound that used to be our car.

The snow at my feet is so loose it churns up as I plough through its dazzling field to check on my precious evergreens. The emergency is worse than I thought. Camellia 'Yuletide' is bent almost double, and a branch has torn off. Wielding the clumsy rake, I reach high to bat snow from the remaining branches. It's embarrassing to disturb the neighbourhood's genteel hush, but I can't help gasping aloud and panting with laughter as each branch springs free and dumps an icy deluge down my neck and up my sleeves.

As I make my way through the garden to check on the other camellias, I'm startled by a set of footprints. They look uncannily human but are only the drifted-in tracks of a bounding squirrel. In the shallow dusting beneath a laden cedar, tiny trident prints tell of towhees, juncos or fox sparrows foraging, their recent journeys written briefly in dainty hieroglyphs. Otherwise, no signs of life. The rest of the snow surface lies unblemished, a pristine page that will record my own travels today.

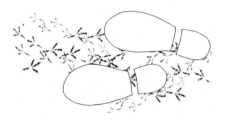

# The Pond

As usual, the snow melted quickly, and now there's a subtle odour of damp earth in the air, an emanation with its own name, petrichor. It's said to induce a sense of well-being, which may explain my pleasantly nostalgic mood as I stroll along the path that runs around the gravel garden, a slightly sunken area that was once a well-loved pond.

Ponds have been important in my life. At ten years old, I moved with my family to a new home in England. The garden had a watery rectangle no bigger than a billiard table at its heart, but what a world was packed into that small concrete tank! I would kneel on the rim with my nose almost touching the water to lose myself, and all sense of time, in the busy life below. Whirligig beetles spun like electrified black beads on the surface, and water striders dimpled it with outstretched legs. Sticklebacks, caddis larvae and diving beetles inhabited the depths, and there were frogs. First came the jelly blobs of spawn punctuated by the small black dots of eggs that grew from periods to commas before they broke free as tadpoles to swim like wriggling sentences along the edges of the pond. Their bodies grew bigger and their tails grew smaller as they sprouted limbs and turned into the froglets that I held briefly in my hand to marvel at their impossibly delicate fingers and toes.

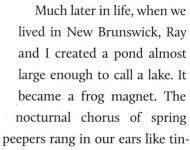

Much later in life, when we lived in New Brunswick, Ray and I created a pond almost large enough to call a lake. It became a frog magnet. The nocturnal chorus of spring peepers rang in our ears like tinnitus, and the chorus of leopard frogs along with the boom of bullfrogs shocked visitors who'd arrived expecting rural peace and quiet.

When we moved west to British Columbia, the garden here had been abandoned for some time and was wildly overgrown. Still, it's hard to believe that we didn't notice for several days that we'd inherited a substantial water feature. Our new pond didn't host any frogs, but we enjoyed it for more than twenty years and so did the dragonflies, damselflies, mayflies, bats, raccoons and bathing robins. Before the growth of surrounding vegetation impeded their flight path, a pair of mallards visited annually to float on the surface like painted wooden decoys.

I like to think of still water as a garden's eye, reflecting the sky's mood, but this pond was no more than an oversized plastic-lined puddle fed by rainwater. The eye was blinkered by a mass of aquatic plants and clouded with cataracts of thick green blanketweed. In summer, the water level sank, and buds of rampant waterlilies stuck up like small, clenched fists. Their leaves, which should have rested calmly on a shimmering surface (Monet comes to mind), protruded and became infested with black aphids. We grew nervous about mosquitoes, so we introduced goldfish, which amused the raccoons and attracted a heron as well as a number of kingfishers before disappearing along the food chain. We also accomplished a couple of magnificently mucky restorations, but the problems became more pressing as summers grew hotter and drier and more rigorous water restrictions kicked in.

Eventually, reluctantly, we decided that the pond would have to go. I did the deed myself. I stood near the edge in gumboots, took a deep breath and plunged a carving knife into the liner. I felt like a murderer. The water drained slowly but eventually, I was able to dig out the deep layer of accumulated sludge and distribute it around the garden, rejoicing in its rich fertility and trying not to think about its wealth of invisible aquatic life. Many wheelbarrow-loads of rocks, broken bricks, road base and pea gravel later, we had a new sitting area — the gravel garden. As an apology to the larger wildlife, I added a bird bath in the form of a scooped-out boulder with a turtle carved into the basin. A miniature pond in memoriam. Our generous neighbour Terry, ever the ingenious forager and capable carpenter, added the perfect gift of a driftwood bench.

I still missed the big pond, and I'm sure that most of the wildlife did too, but the raccoons were delighted. They mistook the turtle pond for a newly installed latrine and demonstrated their approval enthusiastically. They must have performed impressive feats of balance because their aim was perfect. A dome of chicken wire discouraged the visits but also kept the birds away, and as a decorative feature, the whole thing rather lost its point. The following year, I dismantled the raccoon guard and kept my fingers crossed. Happily, the adaptable creatures had moved on by then to less precarious premises.

# Wind

The blustery weather doesn't tempt me outside, so my journey today has taken me no farther than the living room where I'm standing by the window staring at a garden in disarray, remembering another windy garden that existed in another place, at another time.

Ray and I studied together in the north of England, and after graduation, we longed to escape from life in a smoggy city. We took jobs in the Shetland Islands, which lie too far north to fit onto most maps of the British Isles and are often left out altogether or boxed and dropped into a more convenient location close to the Scottish coast. A lengthy and tempestuous overnight sail from Aberdeen demonstrated that our new home did, in fact, lie well detached from the British mainland.

We rented a neat semi-detached house in the village of Scalloway. A family of seven occupied the other half, and it was the mother, Violet, who along with other kindly neighbours, taught me everything I needed to know about the beguiling but baffling Shetland dialect, about the preparation of fish, about knitting and, eventually, about baby care. Each house had a small garden surrounded by wire fencing, and Violet's was a carefully tended patch of potatoes — tatties. Surprisingly, she also grew Peruvian lilies, which she called poor-man's orchids. Our plot was nothing but bare soil and weeds, and I set about it with all the ardour of a first-time gardener.

Shetland is famous for its knitwear made from local wool. The sheep, like the ponies, have to deal with Atlantic gales and are low-slung with shaggy fleeces. They sometimes roamed through the village in small flocks baaing in various octaves like a highly dissatisfied tour group. I was shocked one day to witness these matronly mommas hitch up their woolly skirts and leap nimbly into my newly planted patch. I gained a whole new respect for sheepdogs when I tried to herd them out through the narrow gate. They left behind a few tufts of wool snagged on the fence, and these I gathered up — a novel garden crop — to add to a collection I'd already started. Eventually, I washed the oily wad, carded it with hairbrushes, dyed it with onion skins, spun it very crudely with a spindle and knitted a few rows of it into a small sweater in anticipation of a growing family.

Sheep were a relatively minor challenge to my gardening efforts. The wind proved a far tougher opponent. Shetland lies at roughly the same latitude as Siberia and the tip of Greenland, so you might imagine us enduring frigid winters. Not so. The Gulf Stream moderated temperatures, and relatively tender plants, such as fuchsias, thrived. However, across the almost treeless islands, the unobstructed blast blew straight off three thousand miles of ocean and smacked into anything that dared to stand upright. This included our visitors from the south, who were knocked senseless for several days after stepping off the ferry. The salty blast made noses run and swept away hairdos along with pretensions.

Eventually, we built our own house overlooking the harbour. Even before we moved in, we started to plant trees for shelter, although we knew that as they grew together, the wind would carve their tops off in a smooth aerodynamic curve. At that time, the Forestry Commission provided seedlings of plantation trees such as Sitka spruce. When we put them in, it never crossed our minds that one day we might live in the homeland of these massive evergreens. Nor did it occur to us that such trees might not be the most appropriate choice. Pollen counts from deep beds of peat showed that hazel, birch, willow and alder had grown on the islands long before ancient shifts in climate — and Neolithic humans bearing sheep — had entirely altered the landscape. I wish now that we'd planted a selection of such small deciduous trees to complement the faint remaining traces of that original woodland.

# Women Travellers

I'm sheltering indoors again, still entertained by my go-to travel writers but increasingly uneasy as tale after tale of derring-do pile up on the coffee table. The authors insist on a virility that has me yearning for more female voices. But where are they, the women?

An initial online search for famous travel writers, greatest travel books and top literary trips confirms a serious gender imbalance. A further search, however, turns up a trove of indomitable female adventurers who plod triumphantly along the rugged Pacific Crest Trail, cycle the politically unstable Silk Road, trek with camels across the blistering Australian desert, navigate the entire Trans Canada Trail and survive everything an Arctic river can throw at them. Biologist Caroline Van Hemert, feeling disillusioned with the sterility of her laboratory studies on chickadees, sets out with her partner on a brutal journey through northern wilderness to see the real thing — nature wild and free, 6,400 kilometres of heaven and hell. Brava! Although it crosses my mind that I have chickadees flitting freely in our somewhat heavenly backyard.

There's no doubt that women have the courage and endurance to match the most adventurous male traveller, but something is still out of kilter. Physical safety and societal pressures are issues for many, but domestic ties have always been the greatest barrier between female travellers and the open road.

To look after her ailing parents, Irish travel writer Dervla Murphy postponed her career until she was in her thirties, and even this tireless woman took a break from travelling until her daughter could join her on a hike through the Peruvian Andes. During her many journeys, she was attacked by wolves, robbers and giant cockroaches. She damaged her hip in Palestine, her coccyx and foot in Romania, her legs in Siberia and her ribs all over the place. Yet, when she was interviewed in retirement, she insisted that the most challenging part of her life was her time as a domestic caregiver.

It's impossible to imagine our gritty male adventurer trudging across the open tundra or kayaking Class V whitewater with toddlers in tow or an infant strapped to his chest. Believe me, I understand the challenges of travelling with small children. Before our lives shifted, as so many Scottish lives have, across the Atlantic to Canada, our family grew rapidly. We emigrated with two preschoolers, a baby and twenty-four items of essential baggage. As I juggled pushchairs, carrycots, sippy cups, pureed vegetables, diapers and precious teddy bears, I stared in envy at the solitary airline passengers who whisked about the world with nothing more than a single piece of hand luggage. How briskly they navigated airports! How peacefully they snoozed through overnight flights!

There are certainly daring and determined women out there, but I still ask myself if all these arduous and far-flung expeditions are altogether necessary. It's a pleasure to come across two women writers who feel as I do that plenty of world is available close to home. Rebecca Solnit in *Wanderlust* claims, "The surprises, liberations and clarifications of travel can sometimes be garnered by going around the block as well as going around the world." Writer and illustrator Maira Kalman, who explores her urban neighbourhood on foot, explains that her work is, "…waiting for the unexpected and to be surprised to be walking down the street and not know what I'm going to see and go, oh, a-ha!" Yes, Maira! Now let's see if we can garner a little "oh, a-ha" by going around the garden.

# Oh, A-Ha!

When we put this garden together, we unintentionally created a microcosm of the planet. Today, in the blink of an eye, we can touch down wherever we choose. Asia, for instance, where maples, skimmias, azaleas, andromedas, camellias, viburnums and spotted laurels (which all bear the specific name *japonica*) will set the scene for a pleasant stroll through the Japanese countryside.

With help from the heavenly bamboo, which grows at the corner of the deck, we can nip over to China, where both Stewartia and Chinese dogwood, along with snowbell, tree peony, umbrella pine and many rhododendrons, look very much at home. And if our imaginations are in good working order, we might even catch a glimpse of a panda lurking over there in the little bamboo grove. Do you think?

At the foot of the garden, we can land in Europe, where the great curly leaves of the acanthus will conjure up the sunny

Mediterranean (at least they will later in the year). If you've ever studied architectural history, you'll know that their sculptural forms inspired the ancient Greeks to create the elaborate Corinthian design that tops some of their stately columns.

If, like me, you've never been to Greece, no problem — anemones and cyclamen will set the scene for a picturesque huddle of whitewashed houses spilling down the slope of a rocky hillside bright with flowers. If we sample the leaves of sage or thyme, we'll be able to taste the Mediterranean, and if we run our hands up the lavender or rosemary stems, we'll even catch a whiff of its resinous, herb-scented air.

Back on the deck, when we gaze at Ray's fuchsias and dahlias, we'll be able to pop down to South America and hang out with the Mexican Aztecs or practice our Spanish with a gang of conquistadores. If Latin America proves too hot to handle, we can pick some *Viola labradorica* or cool off beside the *Iris sibirica*. On the way, we might like to drop by several states: *Weigela florida*, *Choisya arizonica* or *Persicaria virginiana*. Fancy a quick trip to New Zealand? Then let's take a look at the neat little boxleaf hebe, native of the Antipodes. The agapanthus and the crocosmia aren't in flower yet, but in a month or two, we'll be able to visit South Africa. Well, by this time, I'm sure you get the picture and might like to catch your breath back here in British Columbia.

# Patchwork

For a week now, temperatures have hovered around both sides of zero with a mix of clear skies, frosty air and slushy precipitation. This morning, part of the deck is basking in pale sunlight while the rest is treacherous with black ice. The driveway has thawed down to the blacktop, but rotting snow still lurks in the shrubby edges. It's become obvious that the whole garden is a patchwork of small climates. Today, warm and shady spots, exposed and sheltered, wet and dry, are clearly visible, picked out in black and white.

When moist soil is partially frozen like this, it sometimes pushes up small columns of ice that are strangely fluted and contorted. I don't know if they have a name, but I do know that fungi associated with dead wood can create even more dramatic extrusions of threadlike ice called frost hair or frost flowers. I make my way to the lower and damper part of the garden to see if the cold spell has made any such magic there.

A pristine forest grew on this land until, a century ago, loggers took out the largest timber. By the time we came to live here, a second-growth forest filled the lower half of the lot. To us, it seemed like a trackless terra incognita, and we called it the jungle. Here, for all I knew, were dragons. Moses-the-cat, who crossed the country with us, led the way as I bushwhacked tentative trails into this overgrown territory and began to poke at the forest soil. Much of it lay in deep shade, but sunlight filtered through in spots, and the ground itself, I discovered, was also a patchwork. For the most part, bedrock lay close to the surface, but its hidden face was far from regular. It plunged erratically down fractured cliffs and, only steps away, thrust back up into domes covered with meagre layers of moss and leaf mould.

A shallow wet area lay at the foot of the jungle. I cleared my way into it and gradually carved away the mucky soil to expose the bedrock in a rough teardrop shape. I hoped this lowest part of the hollow would collect rainwater in a small pool, while its narrower neck would resemble a dry creek spanned by a wooden bridge. Thanks to Ray and our helpful son, the bridge eventually came to be. The pool, not so much. Rain trickled into it as planned, but the rock had hidden fissures, the water seeped away, and I was left with a large sloppy puddle. Fortunately, at the time, I was reading

*The Damp Garden* by renowned garden writer Beth Chatto, and I decided that moisture-loving plants such as marsh marigold, royal fern and Japanese swamp lantern were highly desirable. I hastily dumped soil back into the lowest part and declared it my new bog garden.

There are no ice columns or frost flowers down here today, but I do notice, with a little leap of the heart, that green spears of summer snowflakes are appearing in defiance of the cold.

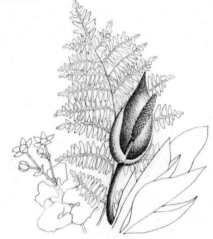

# New Canadians

When I started this project, I imagined I'd simply step outside, enjoy a breath of fresh air and wait until something interesting cropped up. I resolved to take my time, muse a little, satisfy my curiosity. It didn't occur to me that gardens from my past would intrude insistently on my garden of the present, but they do.

We had flown to New Brunswick from the Shetland Islands in March, and I had hoped, in my ignorance, to dance with the daffodils and frolic with the lambs. We were greeted instead by eroding snowbanks and a total absence of green grass. When I think back to the island landscapes, I see them painted in the colours of sea and sky, brisk brush strokes of blue and sparkling white anchored by the peaty browns and misty purples of the hills. These colours hardly changed through the seasons. Colours in Canada's Maritime provinces, I soon discovered, altered dramatically.

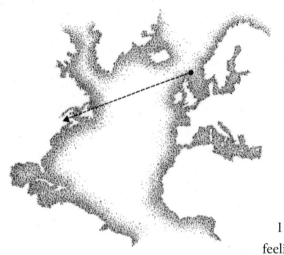

A month or so after our arrival, when we'd almost given up hope, winter came to an abrupt end. The earth trickled, gurgled and gushed into spring, which lasted all of five minutes, and then bam! Next thing we knew, it was full-blown summer.

I spent the following months feeling queasy. Part of the trouble was the sudden switch to unaccustomed heat, but my real problem was the foliage. The stunted alders and the wind-whipped sycamores of Shetland bore no resemblance to the stately elms and lindens that towered over us in our new village home. As these lofty canopies thickened and billowed overhead, it all became too much. It was simply too *green*. I staggered red-faced and faintly nauseous through June, July and August while our neighbour grinned and asked repeatedly, "Hot enough fer yeh?"

The autumn took us completely by surprise. We watched in amazement as our world smouldered, then burst into leafy flames of crimson and gold. No sooner had we accustomed ourselves to this conflagration than its embers faded, and we plunged into our first full-on New Brunswick winter. Our neighbour changed his tune to "Cold enough fer yeh?" We learned about snowploughs and road salt, frozen soil and freezing rain. We also learned that a garden's nemesis was not so much the snow as the lack of it.

Without its protective robe, frost dug its claws in deeply, and the cycles of freeze and thaw ripped roots apart. The garden simply shut down, became a kind of frozen tundra, and I sang along with Quebecois songwriter Gilles Vigneault, "*Mon jardin, ce n'est pas un jardin c'est la plaine.*"

Ruefully, I tossed aside my British gardening magazines, which urged me in all seriousness to grow colour in the winter garden. The season, however, did have its own beauties. Drifts of snow stripped the land to abstracts of seductively curved shadows with leafless shrubs and stalks scratched on in black ink. Sometimes, coats of ice illuminated every twig, and the air itself glittered. True, there was a little subtle colour, but it wasn't exactly vibrant. After our first, long monochrome winter I was ready — more than ready — to welcome the Day-Glo green of grasses that filled the roadside ditches and then spread upward until the air was once again suffused with quivering viridian light. I never again suffered from green sickness.

In the Atlantic provinces, apart from a few exceptionally hardy rhododendrons, we depended on needled evergreens such as junipers and pines for substance in the winter garden. Imagine the difference when we moved to this relatively balmy Pacific coast of British Columbia. All year, we could enjoy greenery that didn't have to cope with either the gales of Shetland or the cold of eastern Canada. An evergreen supermarket.

# Ghosts

We made the big move — *from East Coast to West* — *in the depths of winter.* On a hair-raising journey through the Rockies in an overloaded car with failing brakes, the novelty of icy peaks and avalanche tunnels soon wore off. We breathed sighs of relief when we finally crossed from a landscape prickled with trees as spare as church spires into forests hung about with the ferny fronds of western redcedars.

On this misty morning, as I stand in the heart of the garden, comforting boughs of cedar still drape around me. Previous owners had added a variety of exotic trees to the property, but when we arrived, the land retained a powerful memory of its past. Four large cedars were by far the most imposing reminders of the ancient forest. Jammed in among them were bigleaf maples, Sitka spruce, hemlock, white pine and Douglas fir. I was delighted and proud to discover that we also inherited three arbutus, which I mistook at first for spindly rhododendrons with flaky red bark.

Our family grew tired of me boasting that arbutus are the only broadleaf evergreen trees native to Canada. Sadly, ours, like many in the region, were suffering from fungal infections and constantly shed dead leaves that proved as treacherous underfoot as miniature skateboards. They struggled on for years, looking more and more wretched. After a decade, I wasn't entirely sorry when one by one they put themselves out of their misery.

The white pine simply dropped down dead one windy night. I hadn't known the small yellow cankers on its bark were symptoms of the lethal blister rust. Another windstorm ripped a huge branch off the spruce and left a scar so ragged the whole tree had to be removed. The maples died of either drought or root rot. Nature seemed to be dealing with overcrowding in her own way. Still, even after this purge, the garden was wildly congested. The Douglas fir would also have to go. Now, only five large trees remain, but standing here among their grey silhouettes, I find myself surrounded by many ghostly presences.

Our cedars seem healthy, but in recent years many others in the region have been dying. It's been shocking to watch these magnificent trees, which meant so much to Indigenous people, succumb to a changing climate. When the victims sicken, they turn a lurid ochre before they fade into transparency and become faint reminders of their once-great bulk. One such towering spectre stands on the far edge of our neighbours' property, clearly visible from our kitchen window. The birds have adopted it as a perch, and we've begun to call it the Lookout Tree.

Crows, robins and flickers are the usual lookouts, but on one occasion, I was thrilled to see the dramatic form of a pileated woodpecker clinging to the trunk. Once, a hawk perched in solitary splendour. Once, a couple of Steller's jays hopped from bottom to top as if the tiered branches were rungs of a ladder. Once, a scurry of squirrels fooled around at the very tip. And once, on a breezy day, the wind sent a volley of pine siskins hurtling into the skeletal branches, where they clung like a fresh crop of leaves until another gust whisked them away. This gaunt ghost of cedars past, which saddened us at first, has become an endlessly entertaining feature in our borrowed landscape.

# A Woman with Boots

At lunchtime, *I was still reeling from the shock of a clumsy accident.* I'd been crouching among the hellebores to cut away some of their spent foliage when I sat back on my heels to ease a cramped position. A nasty scrunch told me I'd settled, full weight, smack on top of something juicy. Sure enough, the plump shoots of a peony — one of my beloved woodland peonies — were smashed flat. If your garden fork has ever pronged a prize potato, or if your spade has ever sliced into the pristine flesh of a fat lily bulb, you'll know how I felt. I was as crushed as the sprouts themselves.

*Stop whimpering,* I told myself. *Go prune the hydrangeas!* But all my gardening get-up-and-go had gone.

This afternoon, however, after a comforting bowl of soup, I'm reconciled. The remains of the peony will probably stagger through the summer to rise again another year. And happily, I do have others that I grew from seed, a lengthy but rewarding process. Much as we'd like to, we cannot float above the garden like scuba divers over coral reefs, or hover horizontally as miraculously buoyant and footless as Giotto's angels. Like it or not, we are grounded in our boots and can only do our best to tiptoe through the tulips.

To tell the truth, I don't wear boots in the garden. Hiking shoes are so lightweight, waterproof and comfortable these days, I can't imagine stomping around in heavy footwear. The thought, however, puts me in mind of the revered English gardener Gertrude Jekyll. She famously wrote about her gardening experience, "It has taken me half a lifetime to find out what is best worth doing and a good slice of another half to puzzle out the ways of doing it." Obviously, she was well ahead of the game. Most of us never make it past the "best worth doing" half.

A painting, dated 1920 by Sir William Nicholson, of Miss Jekyll's gardening boots made her footwear almost as famous as she was, and the originals — leather-laced, steel-toed, hobnailed and much repaired — are still on display at Godalming Museum, near her home at Munstead Wood. She was in her forties when she purchased them, and it's said she wore them until she died at eighty-nine. Now that's impressive footwear and an admirably thrifty woman!

I have a shrubrose named 'Gertrude Jekyll,' distributed by breeder David Austin, and its unapologetically pink blooms are stuffed with fragrant petals. I make my way up the driveway to the roadside to see how she's faring. At this time of year, she's only a fountain of thorny branches very much in need of pruning, a job I should have done a month ago. Nearby, coincidentally, is another plant named in Miss Jekyll's honour. 'Munstead' is the large lavender that grows contentedly in dry soil under the eaves in front of the house. It has outlived its "best-before" by many years, but every summer it still flowers profusely and hums with bees. I see it too needs a trim before the new growth starts in earnest. I promise myself I'll get to both the rose and the lavender tomorrow. If I finally finish pruning the hydrangeas. If it isn't raining.

# Signs of Spring

The driveway circles around a bed that features a weeping elm. I'd never have chosen such a freakish tree for the centrepiece, but there it was when we came. I must admit, I'm now fond of it, especially in springtime when it sprigs itself out in fresh leaves. In summer, the tree looks like a giant mushroom and in winter, its bizarrely contorted branches resemble something dreamed up by Dr. Seuss. When I'm working near the road, passersby — the kind who notice things like trees — ask me about this oddity. I tell them with a sort of proprietorial pride how all the Camperdown elms in the world descended from one peculiar seedling. It was discovered by a gardener at Camperdown House in Scotland who, smart fellow, grafted it onto the trunk of a regular Scotch elm, and the rest is history.

The tree attracts a startling array of leaf hoppers, borers and mysterious blue midges that leave it gasping for breath and shedding bits of itself all year round. On the upside, its dense topknot of bizarre branches has often served as a secure nesting site for robins.

Safely corralled at its feet are two vigorous, low-growing plants, *Campanula poscharskyana* and *Campanula portenschlagiana* (but let's just call them creeping bellflowers). Later, I'll enjoy their pretty blue stars, but for now, I'm happy to see some early crocuses and daffodil spears poking up through the soil. I pick a slim white crocus bud and carry it into the warmth of the house, where I place it tenderly in a tiny vase. It promptly springs open to expose its bright orange pistil and anthers. I can't take my eyes off it.

# That Rascally Bird Again

After a session of housework, I'm leaning on the railing of the deck to bask in the sun's gentle warmth. From here, I stare directly into the branches of the star magnolia. A week ago, its swollen buds began to split their silky grey casings and reveal slivers of white inside. Now the flowers are starting to burst loose and soon the tree will become a cumulus cloud of blossom.

There's no sign of bossy Alf on his favourite twig. He's been behaving oddly lately, feeding more twitchily than usual and keeping a constant lookout across the garden. Maybe there are new rivals on the block, or maybe the warmer weather has triggered romantic yearnings. Alf, I suspect, has been feeling the urge to make more hummingbirds. I've watched the mating ritual of these birds, and it's every bit as astonishing as you might expect from their supercharged natures. The aerial event takes place in a gap between the hemlock and a cedar. This particular airy space must work well for Alf's purpose because his performances there have been spectacular.

Anticipation begins when, on a fine day like this, his girlfriend, disguised as a particularly large magnolia bud, settles in her seat. To accommodate small waves of wind, she shifts her weight and rocks slightly like an experienced sailor. Her suitor makes a sudden entrance, orienting himself to blast her with the full sunlit effect of his showy costume, and when he's sure of her undivided attention, he darts off and climbs, up, up, until he's a speck against the dazzle. Higher still. And then he plummets. It's a death-defying dive. He must reach a speed sufficient to send his tail feathers vibrating in an explosive squeal, and then, before he slams into the ground, he must make a U-turn to end up facing her, flaunting his glory once again. I'm not party to what happens after that, but I do know that nest building proceeds apace.

In the shady bed to the north of the deck, the hellebores are now in flower, and a movement among them catches my eye. A female hummingbird is braving the dangers of low-level flight to check out the blooms. Suddenly, she shifts up to investigate flecks of turquoise-coloured lichen on the trunk of the cedar tree. My suspicions about Alf's activities are confirmed. His mate is checking out construction materials.

A hummingbird nest is an entirely female undertaking, a seemingly impossible feat of dexterity. Spider silk is key. Sticky and stretchy, it holds the whole expandable structure together. Our little mother will start with a platform of soft plant fibres, and then she'll use her bill to weave moss into the sides of a cup no bigger than a golf ball. For camouflage or possibly for waterproofing, she'll finish the outside by dabbing on flakes of lichen, and then (I find this part particularly endearing), working as carefully as a potter perfecting a vessel, she'll neaten the rim by hovering and rotating while she squeezes the downy materials between her chin and her chest. All this technique comes from a brain the size of a corn niblet. She'll complete the whole process in less than a week, then incubate her two tiny eggs for another two weeks and proceed with feeding and nest maintenance for a further three weeks until her growing chicks finally spill over and fledge.

Throughout this entire process, I'm sorry to say, Alf will be AWOL, possibly off to strut his stuff elsewhere, possibly off to the pub for a pint. Ah well! I don't suppose he ever claimed to be a paragon of domesticity.

# Fluff

It may be Alf's lady love who is plucking at seed heads of the Japanese anemone today. In summer, I enjoy the pink flowers of this plant, although I'm cautious about its determination to spread. The black roots expand stealthily into the neighbouring soil, and their seeds blow around the garden. I could cut down the stems after they flower, but of course, I don't because any nuisance is a small price to pay if it helps to raise a fresh crop of hummingbirds.

Like the seeds of thistles or dandelions, the anemone fluff will make a soft lining for this busy female's nest. She stuffs her beak until the harvest bulges out like an oversized moustache. I can almost see her mind at work. "Thirsty, need a break!" She flies confidently over to the feeder. "Drink? Oh, yes!" and then, as realization dawns, "Fluff? Oh, no!" She hovers indecisively and leaves disappointed.

Alf and his family are Anna's hummingbirds, a species that has never been migratory. They used to be Californians but took advantage of the changing climate as well as the human readiness to provide them with fuel and expanded their range northward. Now, some live year-round here on British Columbia's southwest coast. A lovely First Nations' story in these parts tells how hummingbirds poked holes in the night sky, and the pinprick perforations became the stars. They must have been rufous hummingbirds, which migrate from the States at this time of year to breed. Hard to believe, but these miniature Americans are even feistier than Alf himself.

# Veggie Patch

When we settled here, we decided that the only way to tackle this overgrown garden was to start at the roadside and work steadily down to the back. Such a sensible approach didn't last for long. Ray was the first to jump the gun. He leapt clear over the front garden, dodged the pond, ignored the jungle and stuck his spade decisively into a strip of relatively tree-free land along the western fence. Here, he announced, lay our new veggie patch.

In retrospect, bedrock protruding from the foot of the slope should have warned him that the area wasn't blessed with the mythological two-spade depth of fertile loam. Undeterred by the discovery that the world itself lay a few inches below the surface, he built up an edge of broken concrete and began to backfill with compost. Since then, countless bins of the valuable stuff have turned the original thin duff into a deep dark substance that we like to think resembles Black Forest cake — but alive.

Today, I've come to see how the patch has overwintered. Swiss chard, kale and collards have survived the frost, and although their outer leaves are riddled with holes, they've been putting on harvestable fresh growth. We don't expect every plant to be perfect. A few remaining leeks are also upright, though wobbly. I should pull them today.

I stoop to pick up a few tea bags lying on the surface of the soil. We are big tea drinkers, and I've always added the spent bags to the compost. A few years ago, however, I noticed that the veggie patch was becoming littered with small squares of grey fabric, and it dawned on me that the original paper had been replaced with something less degradable. I didn't fancy micro-plastics among our organically grown produce, so I've been removing the suspects ever since and now buy our tea from a local company that uses compostable paper.

At the bottom of the patch, raspberries and black currants are waking up, and even more noticeable, rhubarb has erupted into damp red knobs as big as eggs. There's something otherworldly about this plant. The protrusions split open to reveal scarlet-tinged convolutions bizarre enough to fire the imagination. Embryonic brains of aliens about to hatch? Unfortunate intestinal escapes? What covert source of energy, in days as cool as these, enables the tightly packed and fleshy contortions to fan out into giant puckered leaves?

A friend's child fell ill after chewing the top of a stalk, and an elderly aunt's arthritis flared up after she'd sampled my stewed rhubarb. The recommended method of harvesting — forcefully yanking the stems from their resolute clutch on the roots — seems heartless. I tread warily around this plant, yet for all its dodgy characteristics, the fruit, or whatever it is, serves us well. Cut up and frozen, baked into coffee cake, mixed with apple in crumble or blueberries in bluebarb pie, and best of all, made into jam with crystalized ginger, this enigmatic vegetation keeps my sweet tooth satisfied throughout the year.

    With a deferential nod to the expanding foliage at my feet, I back off and head for the house. On the way, I notice that the clumps of chives are tall enough for cutting. Chopped and loaded into cheese bannock, they'll go well with tonight's chowder. We use chives and parsley lavishly, more like vegetables than garnishes. No scurvy lurks in this house.

# Flowers to Make Your Heart Happy

Sunshine, a fistful of roasted cashews and a glass of cider accompany me on my travels this afternoon, but it isn't the bubbles alone that are giving me this buzz, this heady feeling that I might begin to prance about and break into song. I'm celebrating the return of the trilliums — tra-la! They grow at the foot of the garden close to the bench, and I plonk myself down beside them to enjoy these lovely native plants with their three-part leaves and neatly matching, three-cornered flowers.

The weather hasn't encouraged us to sit around outside until now, so I haven't introduced the bench to you yet. When our gardening efforts reached this final frontier, Ray and I stood together feeling slightly stunned. Perhaps for the first time, we turned and looked back up. We could see across the bog garden, up through the jungle, past the star magnolia, over the pond and then all the way up to the tall trees of the park on the other side of the road. This long view reaching across so many years of effort impressed us mightily, and we marked the occasion. Ray built a flagstone base, and we splurged on this useful piece of garden furniture. The original design was by architect Edward Lutyens, who often worked in partnership with Gertrude Jekyll. (Remember the boots?)

Along with the trilliums, anonymous shoots are poking up in a most encouraging manner, and splashes of fresh greenery are racing to grab good sunbathing spots. Windflowers and dainty little starflowers, spring snowflakes, merrybells and hepaticas are all eager to get in on the action.

I crunch a cashew, sit back and relax as a calmer kind of happiness seeps in. Let's feast our eyes while we may! Many of these early flowers are ephemeral. They harvest the sunlight hastily, suck its sustenance underground, then fade away as more overhead foliage blocks the rays. I love to think of them storing away this sunny energy in the dark, waiting for whatever subtle messages will trigger them to pay another whirlwind visit to our upper world of airy breezes and dappled light, our joyful world where everything alive is clamouring to join us in the sweet delirium of spring fever. Sing it, Elvis! Sing it, robins!

Here on the Pacific Coast, we should give thanks every morning in March, April and May that spring is a proper season. In most of Canada, the tulips trip over the snowdrops, the roses trip over the tulips, and the gardeners trip over themselves. Although spring lasts for a full three months here, it still keeps us on the hop. A host of tasks, all equally urgent, are crying out for attention, and I know that I'll never keep up. It isn't only the press of jobs that flusters me; it's the impossibility of appreciating everything at once. I want to greet every old friend and enjoy the swell of every bud, the unzipping, uncoiling, unstoppable emergence of this giddy season.

On my journeys so far, I've managed to dawdle more or less aimlessly and allow my mind free rein to wander, but it's becoming harder by the day. I'm by no means the only traveller to find myself constantly tempted to rush. Dianne Whelan, the first person to complete the entire Trans Canada Trail, described how taking her time was a lesson she had to learn, how eventually she "dropped the rabbit suit and put on the turtle shell." Her proposed *500 Days in the Wild* lasted six years. Six thoroughly fulfilling years.

Perhaps I'm beginning to learn the turtle trick as well because I've decided to sit here for a little longer and commune with the trilliums. I'm certainly not going to jump up, abandon my cider and dash to the greenhouse in a panic just because I've suddenly remembered that my fresh batch of seeded lettuce must be drying out. Oh no, I won't make that mistake again. In my scramble a week or so ago, instead of spritzing the seed trays with water from my handy recycled spray bottle, I gave them a good soaking from an identical bottle of window cleaner left there after a short-lived spasm of greenhouse spring cleaning.

# Surprise!

Casualties occur in any garden. Ponds silt up, trees blow down, snowstorms wreck the camellias, bears destroy the compost bins, and you water the seedlings with window cleaner. In our three decades on this plot of land, our best-laid schemes have gone agley more often than I care to remember. Canadian writer Thomas King, the author of *Indians on Vacation*, claimed that the first expectation of travel stories is that things go wrong. If that's the case, my garden travelogues are on the right track.

In the greenhouse today, however, things went surprisingly right. A little miracle awaited me. After the window cleaner incident, I'd doused everything with water until it puddled on the greenhouse floor and the seeds floated.

Then, I abandoned the whole lot in disgust. To my astonishment, the trays are now hazed with green — lettuce looking perky, leeks starting to pry their tips from the soil, chard going gangbusters and even the slow-to-germinate parsley peeping through. How is this possible? I still expect them to keel over, but if they do survive, they'll certainly be the cleanest crops I've ever grown.

# The World Beneath a Traveller's Feet

When I set out on my journey this morning I didn't bother to change into outdoor footwear, and the gravel surface of the shady path soon impressed on me the painful fact that grit and flip-flops don't mix. As I limped back to the house, I reflected on the world beneath a traveller's feet, a realm that's easy to ignore until a small stone wedges itself under your arch. Robert Louis Stevenson claimed he travelled to "come down off the feather-bed of civilization, and find the globe granite underfoot and strewn with cutting flints." A brave sentiment no doubt, Mr. Stevenson, but I'm not buying it.

Stones of all shapes and sizes play a big role in this garden. I paved the entrance path with irregular slabs of slate. Setting them on a bed of sand was a muscular jigsaw puzzle. My favourite path, however, is laid with cobblestones. At the landscape supply yard that later provided us with the turtle pond, I spotted a dump of old rocks half hidden in a corner. It didn't take me long to look them over. I sidled up to the office and offered to take them off their hands, help tidy up the premises, as it were. I should explain that these were no ordinary rocks. I knew it, and unfortunately, the business manager knew it too. Although I still think of them as cobbles, they are more correctly called setts. Each one is unique, a deep rectangular chunk of granite, quarried, I learned, on Nelson Island up the coast from here.

They'd been individually cut and laid as the first hard-surfaced paving in Vancouver's Gastown, where decades of iron-wheeled, horse-drawn traffic had worn their surfaces to a fine polish. In short, they were magnificent antique artifacts, and I wanted them.

I wanted to feel their heft. I wanted to stroke them. I wanted, with a fierce covetousness, to take them home with me. The manager grinned and named his unnegotiable unit price. I retreated in shock and drove home downcast. The next morning, I was even more downcast, and a few mornings after that I got up early, drove back to the yard, bought every last one and returned home on top of the world and dangerously low in the bank account.

They were rock steady, smooth but never slippery, pleasantly varied in colour and steeped in local history. Soon, with small plants softening the edges and the fine green lines of creeping mint weaving between them, they looked and smelled even more beautiful. If ever I have to leave this place and could take some of the garden with me, I think I'd choose a piece of this path.

# Marvelous Mulch

My bare feet like to linger on the smooth granite of the cobblestones, but they've grown soft since I ran barefoot as a child, and nowadays, they insist on shoes for rough surfaces. Gravel, as I discovered, can be a pain, which is a pity because I like to think of myself as a connoisseur. Crushed rocks, grits and pea gravels in all their rich variety of colours and grades are irresistible. A friend in New Brunswick loved the stuff so much she'd sneak out before daybreak to scoop it up from the sides of the chip-sealed road where snowploughs had shoved it into lateral moraines. I seem to cultivate gritty friends. I wasn't surprised to learn that neighbour Terry, gifted gardener and resourceful recycler (whose bird feeder, you may remember, lost a battle with a bear), has also liberated the odd bucketful from gravel heaps abandoned by the nearby railroad.

Then there are pebbles. They may not be kind on the soles, but is it possible to stroll along a pebbly beach without pocketing a treasure or two? These mementos of hikes and holidays stay hoarded long after they've dulled and lost their significance. Ah, but with a little spit, a little polish, memories may stir, and stones once again become precious gems. White or black, green or tan, mottled, glittery or speckled, silky smooth, shot through with enigmatic scribbles of quartz, round as turtle eggs or flat as tokens — the variety! Imagine the stories they might tell, the journeys they've made to reach here and now. Over the eons, the Earth has mangled and mashed its surface time and time again: swilled it, swallowed it and spewed it out like simmering porridge until only tiny fragments of the original mantle remain. We in Canada can boast one of the rarest of these crusty bits; on the edge of Hudson Bay lies rock more than four billion years old. The pebbles in my hoard have doubtless been crushed, reassembled and ground down many times since then. I struggle to get my head around geological time frames, but a handful of pebbles can help.

Not all our paths are hard-surfaced. Those in the jungle have been through several incarnations. First, there was the forest soil itself, in places shallow and rocky, in other spots deep and muddy. Walking on it was no pleasure. In such a shady area, grass paths were out of the question. Moss would have taken over in no time, so with visions of Japanese gardens dancing in my head, I thought, *Why not let it?* Without a team of dedicated Japanese gardeners on hand, however, the surfaces soon became a patchy mess. Eventually, I saw the light and ordered a truckload of bark mulch.

Finely shredded hemlock bark is the forest's gift to gardeners, which explains why I'm now standing on the driveway gloating over a small Mount Baker of the sweetly resinous material. The pile, as usual, is a large one because, as I explain to Ray, the delivery charge is as high for one yard as it is for three or six or nine, so we might as well go the whole hog, right? Neighbour Terry wonders where all this lovely stuff ends up, and I often wonder that myself. I only know that it goes into the wheelbarrow and is trundled down to wherever it creates more paths or reconfirms existing ones or discourages weeds or makes a warm winter blanket for the plants or keeps the soil moist in the face of ever-increasing summer droughts. Or simply makes me happy.

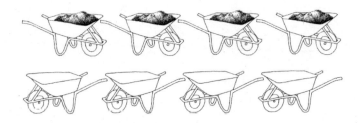

MARVELOUS MULCH

# Eavesdropping on the Birds

Coast Salish people in this part of the world recognize a year of thirteen lunar months relating to the seasonal round of fishing, hunting and gathering. Their various calendars, however, aren't all about hard work. April is the time of blossoming and is sometimes called the Moon of the Whistling Robins. Ray and I have brought our coffee onto the deck and we're listening to our current robin tell us over and over again that this patch of earth is home and that we should, "Cheer up! Cheer up!" And we do.

This bird is probably the son or the grandson of Ridge Robin, who serenaded us from dawn to dusk a number of years ago from the tip of our roof ridge and left us a trail of well-fertilized moss on the cedar shakes. His arrival coincided neatly with the return of the trilliums, which explains why the flowers are sometimes called wake-robins.

Most of the resident birds are busy building nests. The black-capped chickadees are certainly in mating mode, though none have occupied the nest box yet. I learned only recently that their piercing *fee-bee* call is both a territorial proclamation, "This land is my land!" and a come-on, "Hey, sweetie!" The more familiar *chick-a-dee* means, "How's it going, eh?" A few additional *dee-dees* bump up the message to convey, "Bit of a problem here, folks," while a whole string of them warns, "BIG problem!" These birds have some of the most complex vocalizations of any bird anywhere. Much of their repertoire is learned and has distinct dialects that include at least sixteen different twitters, squeaks, snarls, gargles and hisses combined in phrases with endless variations. That sounds a lot like a language to me.

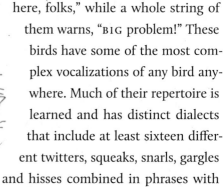

A crow is spying on us from the treetops in the park. Sometimes, when I'm working around the driveway, I chat with any crows or ravens perched there and easily convince myself that they respond. These birds are curious and vocal in ways we humans recognize as intelligence. Research in Seattle some years ago showed they also have good memories as well as remarkable powers of facial recognition (gifts I truly envy) and can even convey their opinions about certain people to their offspring. Unlike them, I'm a poor mimic and, although I give it my best shot, it's hardly surprising that my corvid neighbours stare down at me with pity, or possibly alarm. "What kind of gibberish is this? Steer clear, kids."

As we sip our coffee, a bald eagle traces spirals in the sky. Several pairs nest nearby, and we sometimes hear them calling, but their voices, for such impressive birds, are disappointing. If a wren were the size of an eagle and its voice were amplified to match, what mighty music would pour from the hedgerows! The complexity and haunting beauty of a wren's song played in slow motion takes my breath away.

Down here, a sudden breeze chills the air. Up there, the eagle grows smaller with each revolution. Ray heads for his studio, but I stay outside to listen longer to the arrival of spring in Canada, its waves of sound lapping on the shores of the forty-ninth parallel and rippling northward. To hear it in full voice, I should have been up and out at daybreak. Although the early morning outburst of song is called a dawn chorus, to me it sounds more like an orchestra tuning up, a blend of chirrups and whistles, disorganized but full of anticipation. To the birds, of course, every note transmits vital information. Birds of the same species pick up and forward signals of identity or welcome or warning, but others listen in and may also pass on the messages. The system reminds me of our early days in rural New Brunswick when our telephone was on a party line that, like it or not, kept the neighbourhood up to date on local gossip.

The sky is busy today. A faint honking alerts me to a family group of geese, possibly lesser snow geese heading for Wrangel Island in the Russian Arctic. Honking is a clumsy word to describe their non-stop chatter. Are they excited, anxious, tired, discussing the finer points of navigation? The flock is flying high in a wide wavering > and some of them will be making the long journey north for the first time.

*Veer west, you guys*
  *My turn up front*
    *Keep up, kids*
      *Where's Grandpa?*
        *Lineup back there*
     *Mum, I'm thirsty*
    *Let's play I spy*
   *Mum, I'm starving*
  *Are we there yet?*

The currents of air that lifted the eagle stir the star magnolia and send its petals twirling to the ground. I want to cry out, "Wait! Too soon. I haven't had my fill yet!" But spring's passage is inexorable. A few more days, a few more puffs of wind, and the trickle will turn into a storm. The next act in spring's drama will be underway.

# Sexy Dust

Today's journey brought me no farther than the mailbox (two bills and no new gardening magazines), and I'm standing in the driveway beside a large tree. *Alexandrina* is a type of magnolia known as a tulip tree. I've always admired the elegant goblet shape of her pink flowers but never took the time to look at them closely. Now, in my new role as slow traveller, I pull a slender branch toward me and break off a flower bud. I try to pry it open, but the petals are fleshy and snap off. I've heard they're edible, so why not try a small bite? Mmm! Crisp texture, slightly sweet taste, and surprisingly gingery. With all its petals gone, the remaining structure resembles a bizarre little sculpture with a solid green tower in the centre — the female part — surrounded at its base by a dense ruff of stubby pink stamens that carry the male contribution. Magnolias are among the oldest flowering plants on Earth and appeared before bees and moths, so for pollination, they must have depended on the clumsier attention of beetles or flies. Their reproductive parts had to be sturdy, and one hundred million years later, I see that they still are.

The driveway is sprinkled with the fuzzy husks that enclosed Alexandrina's large buds. Every gust of wind brings a fresh bombardment of biomass — biomess? The sheer quantity of debris that rains down on us throughout the year is astonishing. Autumn leaves, of course, but also petals, needles, cones, seeds, fronds, twigs, berries, tufts of moss, clusters of lichen and shreds of bark. Now I'm shocked to see, in a shaft of low sunlight, that the air is thick with dust motes sifting from overhead. They waft gently this way and that, responding to imperceptible shifts in the currents of air. Not dust, of course, but pollen. Across the road on the edge of the park, the dangling flowers of bigleaf maples are in full swing, distributing their pollen not by way of bee or beetle but by wind.

A clingy yellow film has coated our parked car and has gathered in drifts below the windshield wipers. I've heard pollen is used as a food supplement so, encouraged by my success with the magnolia petals, I dab a little on my tongue. Nothing.

Tasteless it may be, but this pollen is remarkable stuff. Most particles are too small to be seen clearly with the naked eye, yet every speck carries half of the wherewithal to bring about a huge tree or a tiny daisy. The distinctive shapes and durability of the particles have made it possible to detect vegetation that grew thousands or even millions of years ago, which informs us of long-term changes in climate and vegetation. They stick to almost anything, including skin and fabric, a trait useful in forensics but also a nuisance, as you'll know if you've ever tried to remove lily pollen from your clothing. It sticks to nasal passages too, a bane for anyone suffering from hay fever.

I walk to the front of the house where, years ago, Ray mounted boxes for mason bees, the little blue-black insects known to be super pollinators. Every year, a female bee deposits a series of eggs in one of the new cardboard tubes we provide. After laying the first egg, the busy mother provisions it with pollen and seals its chamber with a mud partition. She then proceeds with laying, provisioning and constructing, followed by laying, provisioning and constructing until the tube is full. Somehow, these astonishing creatures arrange it so the last eggs she lays will be males. These, the first to emerge as adults, will hang around until the new females catch their first breaths of fresh air. A quick how-do-you-do and that's it. Their manly work is over.

SEXY DUST

# A Clamorous Cacophony of Colour

No need, these days, to stand about waiting for my senses to tell me that something's afoot, no need to prick up my ears or sniff the air. A garden engages all the senses, but in this colourful month of May, the visual blast is everything. Gone are the demure halftones and pale pastels of late winter, the sprightly creams and blues of April. Tulips sing out in vibrant reds and yellows, purples and oranges. The soles of my shoes are clogged with sticky sepals cast off by a thousand rhododendron blooms. The driveway is paved with magnolia petals, the paths awash with crimsons and pinks of camellias.

As gardener-in-chief, I'm supposed to conduct this exuberant performance, but I make a bewildered maestro at the best of times. With the players stepping up in dizzying succession, I'm ready to throw in the baton, stagger off the podium and let them have at it with their own allegro version of *The Rite of Spring*. Outstanding in this multicoloured mayhem are the many rhododendrons left to us by the previous occupants. Currently leading the percussion section and brazenly out-clashing wind and strings is *Rhododendron augustinii*, a variable species. Clones have been selected for their various shades, from wispy mauve to deep violet, but this one is a flat-out, thumping purple. This imperial shrub now reaches the eaves of the house, overpowers the entrance path and fills the studio with a strange light that grows eerily more intense at dusk. Even delivery men have stopped to take photos.

Nearby, rhododendron 'Starlet' flaunts an eye-popping garb of Hollywood pink, competes with Augustus for attention and mocks the more delicately tinted blooms of *Rhododendron williamsianum* across the gravel garden. William with his neat, rounded leaves and bell-like flowers, arrived here as only half a shrub, donated by a friend whose attempts to control weeds with a flame-thrower went spectacularly awry. Soon, poor William will also be upstaged by 'Vulcan' who'll stride onto the scene blaring fiery trumpets. Accompanied originally by a blood-red 'Vincent Van Gogh' and a flaming 'Cavalier,' 'Fireman Jeff' failed to extinguish the conflagration, and perhaps fortuitously, all three burned out over the years.

I'm just as greedy as any other gardener, and although I wouldn't dream of adding *Pieris japonica* 'Mountain Fire' or 'Forest Flame' to this incendiary mix, I can't resist those oh-so-tempting rhododendrons that come in tawny oranges and salmony pinks. I've kept a slipshod inventory of my plant purchases over the years and even a quick glance through it exposes the embarrassing number of plants that have passed through my hands. I wouldn't dream of adding purchase prices, but I do, whenever I remember, make a note of arrivals and departures. X marks a passing. Reading through the list is an emotional blend of pleasure, guilt and nostalgia, much like browsing through an old photo album, an address book, or nowadays through "friends" on social media. Who on earth were they? Where are they now? Many, like X 'Fireman Jeff' and his X pals, dwell in some heavenly rhododendron garden, and I'm a little put out to see that even X Elspeth departed along the way.

# The Merry Month

I *should be doing something useful like transplanting the tomato seedlings, but on this glorious May morning, I am instead gazing at a woodland peony, sibling of the one I crushed earlier this year. I hesitate to suggest that I have garden favourites, so I'll lower my voice while I tell you about this plant.*

The plant I'm adoring is, according to horticultural literature, a knee-high clump of segmented leaves with white flowers on sturdy stems, referred to as the inverted egg-shaped peony. Clump? Sturdy? Inverted egg-shaped? What kind of description is that? These lightly fragrant, immaculate chalices with their virginal petals cupping bosses of adorably red-tipped styles (take a breath!), arranged neatly in exquisite frills of golden stamens set among elegantly formed, dusky leaves bearing drops of rain like tiny beads of mercury are (another breath!) perfection. Perfection. As if all these virtues weren't enough, the seed heads are also extraordinary, and I promise to describe them later in the year when they're at their showiest.

As with any peonies, the flowers don't last long, but for me, their fleeting loveliness is part of the appeal. I'm not suggesting that all long-lived flowers are unworthy. The almost perpetual blooms of butterfly orchids, for instance, are a gift to home decor, and I grow some of my own. I'm only saying that I sometimes feel I should be dusting them, that less can be more, that ageing has its own beauties, and that I'll never be tempted to leave home on the few days when the woodland peonies are in bloom.

More peonies are already adding to the current outbreak of loveliness. A few spots of overnight rain sparkle on the small, deep red globes of the cut-leaf peony, while the white tree peony is starting to puff out in a stunning display of frou-frou extravagance. A description of its bursting buds as balls of silk heavy in the hand has stuck in my mind. Maybe the writer was Eleanor Perenyi, whose 1981 book *Green Thoughts* has mysteriously disappeared from my shelves. Maybe it finally fell apart.

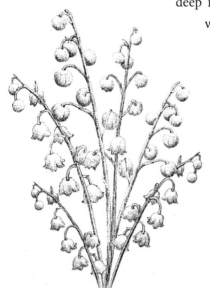

I drag myself away from the peonies to visit a patch of lily of the valley that thrives in the jungle. More than thrives. This small plant seems intent on taking over the neighbourhood, but still, I can think of worse things than backyards filled with these deliciously scented flowers. For centuries, the French have presented lily of the valley as a gift on the first of May, the Fête de Muguet, so perhaps it's time for me to start my own Fête de Muguet tradition by giving small bouquets to my friends.

With my serotonin levels thoroughly topped up, I'm now tripping lightly around the gravel garden singing snatches of English folk songs. If such old ditties weren't about yuletide they were usually set in this merry month when spirits were blithe, the greenwoods gay, the dews dewy, the birds gladsome, the ploughmen jolly and the milkmaids invariably pretty.

*We were up long before the day-o / To welcome in the summer / To welcome in the May-o…*

I'm not sure about the words, so I find myself trying to whistle instead, a skill I've never mastered. It goes with a happy-go-lucky attitude, which is probably why many societies have frowned on it, especially in relation to women. A laughably sexist saying claimed that a whistling woman and a crowing hen would never come to a good end, but perhaps if we all learned to whistle again, like ploughboys or gypsy rovers or like easygoing women, we'd be less stressed by this modern world. So, I say, go for it, hens. Crow up a storm. Whistle your happy hearts out. In the meantime, I'll have to settle for my own wheezy efforts and for Robin who is pouring *his* heart out into the carefree air above my head.

# The Buzz

Bee Day falls on the twentieth of May. I'm so wary of being coerced into celebrating random "Days" that I'm ready to join those celebrating a Day of Non-Observances. Nevertheless, I've found myself hanging about on the deck this week watching bees on the blueberry bush that grows here in a large pot. In today's late-afternoon sunshine, the small urn-like flowers have attracted half a dozen bumblebees. Their attention to every bloom explains the good fruit set, which surprisingly provides as many berries as I can be bothered to pick, even with the help of the towhees.

One of the bees is huge, black and furry with a yellow head and a single yellow stripe — an airbus among the single-engine turboprops. Although Ray insists it's a lance corporal, more reliable sources suggest it's a yellow-faced bumblebee native to British Columbia and an important pollinator in commercial agriculture, especially for greenhouse tomatoes. Working bumblebees in greenhouses?

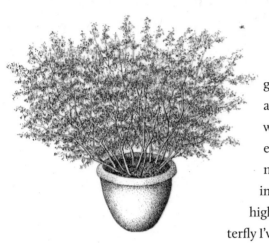

The native crabapple tree, which grows near the veggie garden, is another bee magnet. Its tiny red buds, which a couple of weeks ago speckled every twig, burst open almost overnight and whipped the whole tree into a froth of creamy white. Perched high among the blossom, the first butterfly I've seen this season is gently opening and closing its wings. Is this little beauty enjoying the sun on its back as much as I'm enjoying it on mine? Is it a tortoiseshell? A painted lady? I'll try to remember to look it up, but I won't go indoors yet on such an inviting afternoon. Instead, I amble down to the foot of the garden and sit on the bench.

I'd forgotten how relaxing a balmy warmth can be, and I let my eyes slide up to rest on the neighbours' tall cedar. The tree is looking sparse, and I'm idly wondering how many more hot summers it'll endure when it dawns on me that the space in front of it is full of moving specks. I refocus my eyes. More pollen? No. This time, the shifting motes are tiny creatures. I see only those that are backlit by the low sun and stand out against the dark branches, so I have no idea how much higher and wider this column of life extends. Some of the larger dancing dots shine brightly enough for me to make out wings — moths, beetles, flies. A few are on a mission, but most appear to be milling about, zigzagging and eddying for no apparent reason. Some of them must be tiny spiders because now and then, the light catches a gleam of gossamer streaming from the treetops. Am I watching some kind of epic dispersal? An aerial love fest?

This living swirl delights me, although I must admit I haven't always felt so uplifted by insects. Both in Shetland and New Brunswick, our gardening efforts were plagued by midges, blackflies and a series of other airborne armies that seemed hell-bent on eating us alive. We were astonished to discover that biting bugs are rarely an issue in this British Columbian coastal garden. Outdoor meals are a pleasure, and we can smell the roses unfiltered through clouds of repellent. In this province, about twenty thousand insect species have been named, and there are probably half that number again, yet very few of them take an interest in us.

This glimpse into the vastness and variety of the aerial world isn't only entrancing, it's deeply comforting. Insects have been making the news lately for all the wrong reasons. Bees, we know, are in trouble. We hear about them because we depend so directly on their efficient pollination for much of our food. We hear less about the decline in other insect populations, although its impact would be equally dire in the long run. Already birds are suffering.

The mesmerizing overhead dance starts to fade and flicker as the sun shifts lower in the sky. The day cools, but I stay seated, my mind suspended between pleasure and a nagging anxiety. Half an hour later, I pry myself up and stroll back to the deck. As I walk past the blueberry bush, I see the bees are as busy as ever.

After some research, I decide that the butterfly on the crabapple tree was a painted lady. These fragile creatures make migratory journeys every bit as astonishing as those of the more famous monarchs. European ladies fly in relays of several generations from Africa to northern Europe and then make single return flights catching lofty air currents and arriving tattered but able to breed and restart the cycle. American ladies are equally adventurous. They take about six generations to make the round trip between Mexico and Canada, sometimes travelling in swarms vast enough to be detected by weather radar. I feel honoured to share today's expedition with a traveller taking part in such an epic journey.

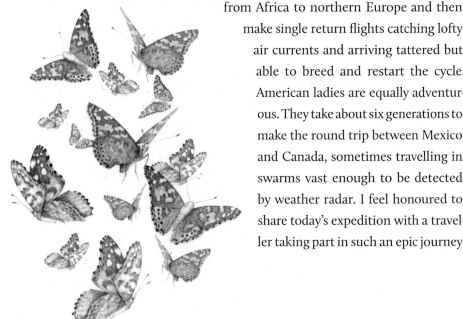

# Frondescence — Fron...What?

**T**hanks to a chance encounter in the Merriam-Webster *Dictionary*, I now have the perfect word to report on the leafy surge that has taken over the garden. This year's vigorous *frondescence* has turned my journeys into obstacle courses. I carry clippers with me as I push my way through rampant new growth, duck under moisture-laden boughs, and stride across encroaching runners that are swallowing the paths. After the multicoloured blast of May, this enthusiastic greenery is fine by me. There's nothing dull about jade, mint, olive, pistachio, emerald and sage, to say nothing of bottle, Hooker's, forest and racing car. Green sickness is a distant memory.

Burgeoning foliage has engulfed the wilted leaves of daffodils on the roadside bank where I'm standing, and the shrubroses have expanded into a thicket solid enough to conceal a sasquatch, let alone the towhees who may be nesting there. Although the roses have yet to flower, the bank looks vibrant, and I take some

credit for that. A number of years ago, I added the slaty purple of an elderberry, the pewter of a red-leaf rose, the dark maroon of coralbells, and the sooty patterns of geranium Samobor. These shades recede like introverts into their background, so I livened them up with the most extrovert foliage colours I could find — lime, lemon, gold and chartreuse. Am I boasting? Why yes! How often do our garden schemes turn out the way we'd hoped?

It's fun to play with coloured leaves, and I also like to fiddle with finely textured, leafy tapestries. This kind of horticultural embroidery is all very well, but gardening is hard work and sometimes the morale needs a boost. That's where the big fellows come in, where frondescence on a grand scale renews the sense of empowerment.

If we stroll down to the damp shade of the jungle, we can admire some impressive foliage. In the bog garden, the tall stems of royal fern have tipped back their clenched fists and hurled their huge fronds into summer. The well-named umbrella plant takes over a good chunk of real estate nearby, and acanthus flaunts its great ornate curlicues. Martagon lilies thrive down here and seed themselves so generously, I wonder if they're halfway to becoming weeds. The muted colours of their Turk's cap flowers are lovely in an underplayed, hellebore way, but it's their leaves, which grow in splendid whorls around the shoulder-high stems, that add substantial drama. Hostas, of course, are stalwarts of imposing greenery. Some, like the gloriously glaucous Siebold's hosta, have expanded from zero to enormous in less than a month. Am I shrinking and sinking like Alice in Lewis Carroll's *Alice's Adventures in Wonderland*?

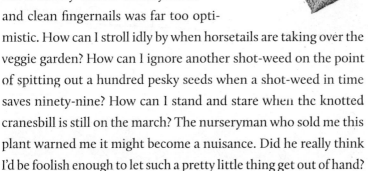

I like to imagine I'm in charge of selecting the plants inhabiting this garden, but with growth in overdrive, I'm struggling. Given half a chance, some residents try to take up far more space than their fair share, and I now know my plan to travel slowly with a dreamy smile and clean fingernails was far too optimistic. How can I stroll idly by when horsetails are taking over the veggie garden? How can I ignore another shot-weed on the point of spitting out a hundred pesky seeds when a shot-weed in time saves ninety-nine? How can I stand and stare when the knotted cranesbill is still on the march? The nurseryman who sold me this plant warned me it might become a nuisance. Did he really think I'd be foolish enough to let such a pretty little thing get out of hand? He did. I was. And it did.

It takes decades of blunders, probably more than a lifetime's, to learn caution. An anonymous green sprout appears. Something rare and delightful? You pamper it and then another one pops up — another and another — and eventually you question a friendly biologist. "Helleborine," he tells you. "An invasive orchid." You have to wonder what the world is coming to when you can't trust an orchid.

# Embracing the Weather

It isn't raining cats and dogs or even (in this multilingual community) buckets, ropes, sheets, spades, stair rods, nails or frogs. But it is raining steadily. I stand in the covered porch feeling wan and uninclined to venture out in such discouraging weather. In Scotland, my sun-challenged native land, there are dozens of fine distinctions between a mere *smirr* and an outright *blatter*. Today's rain falls somewhere in between. It gurgles in the downpipes and taps like impatient fingers on the deck.

Alexandra Horowitz, in her book, *On Looking: Eleven Walks with Expert Eyes*, tells how one of her experts, a visually impaired man who navigates with a cane, can also use the tap of raindrops to pinpoint his location. For such a skilled listener, the pattering on various surfaces and at different heights or distances must be like hundreds of additional cane tips rounding out his "view" of the surroundings. I close my eyes in an effort to "see" this three-dimensional sound picture. Maybe it works — just a little?

I wonder suddenly why I'm cowering here like a wimp. My fellow travellers, who report on some of the Earth's most challenging environments, wouldn't dream of letting a few drops of water stand between their wanderlust and the open road.

Right. I shall sally forth and embrace the weather.

I've now sloshed my way down to the bog garden, where I'm standing on the bridge, peering through a streaky veil. If I ignore the raindrops falling on my head, I can focus instead on the fat droplets that dangle from the tips of every twig. They tremble and quiver and plop onto the plants below where they shatter into glistening beads. Nice. The water has turned the bog into a pool, and its surface spits and seethes. Those concentric ripples, all those rings that collide in a frenzy of expansions…are they intersecting? I stare for a long time, and yes, they are. For a closer look, I clamber down carefully onto a slippery rock. But what's this? Among all the watery commotion, my swamp lantern is a sorry mess of tattered leaves. Slugs have been out in force overnight and here they are in broad daylight still clinging to the dripping shreds.

So what will I do about it? Not much. I've been battling these creatures for years, and I'm ready to call a truce. I've lost the will to come out on patrol at dawn and dusk. Neighbour Terry takes scissors with her on such expeditions, but that "ugh factor" is too high. Nor shall I bother with the beer traps, copper bands and crushed eggshells I once fussed over. I used to beg spent coffee grounds from the puzzled but obliging counter staff at our local Starbucks until someone on high decreed that the precious stuff be mixed in with their trash. A few years ago, after far too long an interval, I dragged myself off to the hairdresser, plucked up the courage to ask for the trimmings and came away with shorter than usual hair and a plastic bag of offcuts. To my surprise, these did indeed fend off some zinnia marauders, so maybe it's time for another trim.

I'll never forget my first encounter with the aptly named banana slug. Even Moses-the-cat seemed awestruck. I've read that these giant West Coast gastropods prefer their food to be a little less than fresh, and it's true they do a better job cleaning up in the park than some dog owners do. It isn't fair to tarnish the reputations of all slugs just because a few are notorious lettuce eaters. We're told they play their part in a balanced ecosystem, so I suppose it's time we learned to live and let live.

Drenched — *drookit*, or *mouillée comme une soupe* — I turn my back on the swampy slugfest and squelch back to the house to change into dry clothes and do something about a leak in the greenhouse roof. Wouldn't you think a thorough soaking and a swampy slugfest would have dampened my spirits, left me downhearted? On the contrary, I feel refreshed and buoyant, positively perky. It's wonderful what the great outdoors and a bit of a hair wash can do for flagging spirits.

# Gardening the Long Way Round

I'm in the greenhouse contemplating the kale seedlings that are long overdue for planting when a cabbage-white butterfly flits in to investigate. If you've ever grown plants of the cabbage family, you'll know about this insect. Its eggs hatch into tiny green caterpillars with voracious appetites. We used to grow broccoli, and no matter how carefully I examined every head before cooking and serving, a small, bleached corpse would turn up on the edge of someone's dinner plate. Now we grow winter broccoli instead and harvest it in early spring before the inevitable competition arrives. White or otherwise, a butterfly is still a butterfly. I guide the intruder gently to the greenhouse door and return to the job on hand. To encourage the kale's rapid growth, I use a weak solution of fish fertilizer. I pour it into my green watering can and give it a good stir. Just as a favourite trowel or pair of clippers may seem indispensable, this green can is my favourite. It once had a red twin that came to a sticky end, and I still mourn its passing.

Please bear with me as I digress for a moment.

I once read a book about housekeeping. I've no idea what prompted me to choose such a subject when I could have been cycling through Ireland with travel writer Eric Newby and his hilariously straight-talking wife, Wanda, or chortling my way through the Appalachians with Bill Bryson and his woefully ill-equipped friend Katz. I can't even remember the title of my unlikely choice, nor can I remember anything about the content except that housekeepers come in two types: the methodical ones who clean an entire room at one time and always do the wash on Monday, and the opportunistic ones who, on the way to do the laundry, dust the stair rail with yesterday's socks. I've never, ever used dirty socks as dusters — not that I remember — but all the same, I place myself firmly in the opportunist camp.

It seems to me the housekeeper classifications also apply to garden-keepers. Type One decides to plant a new rose and plants it. Type Two is in the kitchen making coffee but remembers the new rose should be planted sooner rather than later and, on the way to find the spade, notices the lilies need staking and pops into the greenhouse for canes, which live beside the bag of lime, so why not drop it off at the veggie patch where the spade is lurking by the peas, which are urgently in need of picking, but the bowl is back in the kitchen along with the string for the lily — and might this not be a good time for that coffee after all? I suspect, however, that both Types One and Two are likely to end up with a planted rose, a staked lily, a bowl of peas and a coffee, though not necessarily in that order or even on the same day.

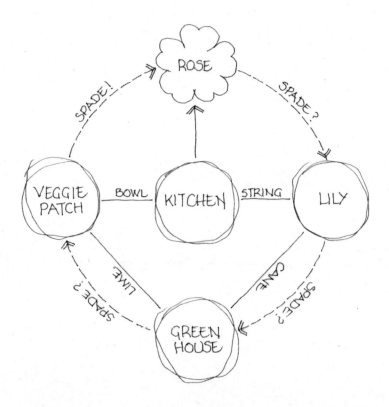

All this is a roundabout way of explaining why the red watering can, along with its fishy contents, stayed outside overnight in the veggie patch, where it shouldn't have been, and why I discovered it two days later, flattened and punctured with dauntingly large tooth marks. It may also help to explain why this travel report has taken such a circuitous route to bring us back to the greenhouse where the kale is still waiting to be transplanted.

I stir the fish fertilizer with care. Fresh in my mind is another accident. Dressed in my best for a long-awaited business meeting, and with a little time to spare, I nipped into the greenhouse to make up a fresh batch of fishy goodness. Discovering that the jug of pungent concentrate was almost empty, I added water, quickly screwed the lid back on and shook the whole thing vigorously. Too quickly. Too vigorously. The top flew off, and a generous fountain of brown goo spurted up, splashed into my hair and ran down the front of my good jacket.

# Oh, Deer!

Neat impressions in the soft earth at my feet are unmistakably the cloven hoof prints of a deer. After thirty years of carefree, deer-free gardening, our luck has finally run out.

I rush to check on the veggie patch. Surprisingly, the green beans, Swiss chard and peas are all present and correct, but a deeper inspection of the garden soon reveals that the picky animal has searched out and destroyed my beautiful hostas. 'Halcyon'? Chewed to the ground. 'Francee'? Salad. Even the huge, slug-resistant leaves of Siebold's hosta have been sampled.

I'm stumbling back to the house in shock when there, smack in the middle of the path, stands the culprit herself. We freeze and eye each other. She is smaller than I imagined. Big soft ears. Long eyelashes. Utterly disarming. She gives me a look of gentle enquiry, and immediately my outrage starts to melt. But a scrap of Hosta 'Golden Fanfare', one of my best, is dangling from her lips, and after a long pause, I manage a half-hearted, "Shoo!" Puzzlement on her part. I flap my hands. "Go, go!" She flicks her tail and chews thoughtfully. Feeling foolish, I pick up a small stone and toss it at her feet. Her expression, I swear, turns from mild surprise to pity. After all, what is the good of chasing her away? I can't patrol our patch day and night, and I really don't want to own a large dog any more than I want to spend a fortune on two-metre-high fencing. Eventually, with a sigh, I turn away defeated, and she also turns, picks her way daintily through the shrubbery and disappears.

Back indoors, I check online for deer deterrents and find a bewildering number of possibilities. I use them all, except for Murphy Oil Soap, because I don't know what it is, and ammonia because I don't have any. I use window cleaner instead and whip it up with powdered garlic, disinfectant, scented liquid hand soap, baking powder, corn oil and beaten egg yolks. I pour some of this witches' brew into a spray bottle and head out in a last-ditch effort to save some of my most susceptible deer fodder. After a few squirts, the nozzle clogs up — no surprise there — and I end up splashing the stinky stuff with a spoon over the weeping Japanese maples.

These telltale hoof prints mark a whole new era for us here. We are not, however, entirely beginners when it comes to gardening alongside grazing animals. When we lived in the Shetland Islands, sheep ate everything bar daffodils. In New Brunswick, porcupines enjoyed our newly planted orchard and then took to gnawing on the deck. Our cabbages were particularly splendid until the groundhogs carefully chewed the top half off each one. In Europe, so I've heard, flocks of wood pigeons peck at anything from cauliflowers to lilacs. Australians cope with far too many rabbits and a million camels. Africans deal with marauding elephants and chimpanzees. Indians…but I'm starting to sound like the Irish Rovers, so I'll stop before we get to unicorns.

The point is that gardeners everywhere have their challenges, and game-changing though this deer may be, I shouldn't complain about an amiable animal with a sweet face. If I have to exchange a few hostas for the entertainment value of more wildlife watching, I can live with that, I tell myself.

When I wrote that last paragraph, I had no idea that our wildlife watching would become quite so game-changing so quickly. Ray was having breakfast when he heard bumping on the deck outside.

OH, DEER!  115

Wondering who could be visiting so early, he opened the door and met a large black bear standing on tiptoe to guzzle nectar from the hummingbird feeder. The feeder, of course, has had to go. Luckily for the birds, there are plenty of flowers around, at least for now, but how I shall miss Alf and his harem!

# The Charm of Chickadees

I'm standing under the simple pergola that marks the entrance to the house and garden. For years, I tried to coax a clematis, 'Hagley Hybrid', to grow over the crossbeam spanning the path here. The name of this vine comes, I imagine, from Hagley Hall in England, but a more genteel honorific would suit her better. Something like 'Lady Grey.' She presents her pinkish-mauve flowers with a formality reminiscent of polite conversation served with afternoon tea in porcelain cups — definitely not a vine for anyone who craves brash colours or who, I discovered, expects compliance from their plants. "Grow across that knotty old beam?" The aristocratic Hagley would have none of it. She made her way instead through the neighbouring red-leaf rose. I must admit, she chose the perfect companion for support, and I half expect her to murmur in the deceptively dulcet tones of Maggie Smith playing the Dowager Countess in *Downton Abbey*, "My dear, I told you so." To this day, the beam remains bare. I know when I've been outclassed.

Years ago, on one of the pergola posts, Ray put up a nesting box for chickadees and, following online instructions, added wood shavings as staging to attract prospective customers. The birds were every bit as stubborn as the clematis. They strongly disapproved of his taste in furnishings and spent several days hauling out every scrap. Since then, we've watched generation after generation of chickadees fledge. This spring, however, the box remained untenanted.

A few weeks ago, as we stood on the entrance path, we noticed a pair of chickadees looping around us in their characteristic scalloped flight. Unphased by our presence, they worked their way closer, and the following scene was unmistakably that of a young couple house hunting. One of them (the female?) flew to the box and perched on the roof. She hopped from side to side, hung over the edge and checked the underside while her partner looked on anxiously. Having thoroughly inspected the structure, she peeped inside. We held our breath. Would the accommodations pass muster? She entered, stayed for a moment, popped out and was gone.

They returned the next day with fresh bedding. For a time, all fell quiet, and we wondered if there'd been a change of heart.

Eventually, however, the to-and-fro of feeding began. It has picked up pace since then, and their tireless efforts make me wonder how many babies are now jammed in there with gaping beaks pleading to be fed. Chickadees can lay as many as a dozen eggs, and the subsequent child care must be exhausting. When I'm in my studio, I catch, from the corner of my eye, the flicker of their comings and goings, and I've grown fond of these hard-working little parents with their invisible brood.

The nesting box is almost embedded in the rose bush, so the chickadee nursery must be infused with a soft pink light filtering through dusky leaves and Hagley's blooms. When the hatchlings poke their heads out, their first impression of the wider world will be a flower big enough to overflow their field of vision. For a chickadee-eye view, I lean in and bring my face close to a handy flower — oh my goodness, the intricacy! The petals (they are properly called sepals, but they'll always be petals to me) have a crystalline texture that adds to their refinement. The dark centre becomes a marvel of complexity, a cluster of maroon-tipped stamens splayed and flattened into a star. I've passed this plant a thousand times, I've noted her underplayed elegance, her obstinate character, but never have I seen her like this.

Last winter, Ray scrubbed out the chickadee nesting box with bleach to get rid of any hidden mites, and I've been wondering if that's why it remained empty for so long. I know a bird's sense of sight differs from our own, and now I'm wondering about their sense of smell. Thanks to Google, I learn that some birds have a keen sense of smell. Seabirds such as albatross can detect marine food at vast distances. Nocturnal birds are also champions. Kiwis, for instance, can sniff out worms in the dark. Juncos preen using oily secretions with either male or female odours strong enough to influence their reproductive success. I'm about to clamber out of this rabbit hole when a stray tidbit of information brings me neatly back to the chickadees. It seems that their European cousins, the blue tits, refuse to enter a nesting box if it retains the faintest whiff of weasel. As usual, one question leads to another, and the next in line is, of course, do weasels smell like bleach?

# Hello, Summer!

We are now well past the solstice. There are those, including my sun-loving daughter, who welcome that date as the start of summer and give heartfelt thanks for the onset of hot weather. For me, however, this time of year is always touched with regret, with a sense of decline. The anticipation and freshness of spring are over. Robins have fledged, hummingbird babies have flown to higher elevations, ferns have unscrolled, and tender foliage has lost its innocence. The frondescence, that great outpouring of springtime energy, is running out of steam — and so am I. My gardening to-do list has stagnated.

I should give myself a shake. Our daughter is quite right to celebrate this gloriously abundant season, and from now on, I intend to join her in savouring every moment of it, which is why I've come to the roadside bed this early morning with my nifty Japanese clippers and a bucket half-filled with water.

This bed is too shady for the tall regal lilies that grow here, but here they remain in the hope that neighbours will be swept up in their heady perfume and give thanks for the gift of life. As far as I know, this has yet to happen. It's also too shady for 'Gertrude Jekyll' and the other roses I planted here, and every winter I decide to replace them with something more suitable, and then every summer I rediscover that I need them, so here they remain as well. Their fragrance seems to evoke a sense of nostalgia even in people who've never had the chance to experience it before. When presented with a truly rosy-smelling bloom, they take a tentative sniff, then draw a deep breath, close their eyes and murmur as if trying to remember something long forgotten.

The sun is already bright, and I bring the bucket, now filled with a haul of loveliness, to work in the shade of the table umbrella on the deck. One of my most treasured possessions is a crystal rosebowl that belonged to my great-grandfather, Thomas. He lived in a small Scottish town, sported a ginger beard, played bass drum in the local pipe band, and according to family lore, consistently won trophies in the annual flower shows. His bowl is fitted with ingenious wire mesh and loops that make flower arranging a cinch.

My expanding floral composition begins to remind me of the seventeenth-century Dutch floral paintings in which voluptuous roses, mysteriously mixed with spring-flowering tulips, burst into such full-blown gorgeousness that a few petals are obliged to fall and lie perfectly placed on the table below. Soon petals will drop onto our own dining table in a fragrant and flagrant display of luxury, and we'll fancy that we live the good life of wealthy *burgemeesters*.

I carry my creation into the house as proudly as if it were a crown. Look, great-grandfather, do you approve? He notices the blemish of black spot on a leaf — this is not a man to be easily impressed — but I catch him smiling behind his beard. The extravagant scent and sultry colours along with his blessing have done the trick. I'm now thoroughly and happily ensconced in the maturity of summer, no longer hankering after spring's naïveté. Elder daughter, you'll be happy to hear that I'm about to dig out the sunscreen, sun hat and shades, loosen my imaginary stays and abandon myself to the glories of the season. Bring on the zinnias!

I was so absorbed in gathering my bouquet of roses, I hardly noticed I'd hooked myself on a thorn. Now, feeling grouchy, I'm nursing a painful thumb.

Ne'er a rose without a thorn! Many poets and philosophers, probably too many, have had a stab at that discouraging theme. John Lydgate, a monk born in 1370, seems to have kicked the whole thing off with, "There is no rose Spryngyng in gardeyns, but ther be sum thorn."

Brother John's inventively spelled insight might have been true in his day but now, thanks to careful breeding, many thornless versions are available. Why, I ask myself, didn't I plant some of those? And while I'm in a cross and picky frame of mind, I'd like to point out that roses don't even possess thorns, which botanically speaking, are sharp stems. Instead, they have prickles that grow out of the bark and are, believe me, every bit as nasty.

# Rebooting the Brain

It's time to visit the spiral patio. More than half a year has gone by since my journeys began, and I still haven't reported on this clearing in the heart of our well-wooded garden. I designed it as a circular terrace outlined with a ring of cobblestones that curl into the centre. Ray built the concave wall of mortared fieldstone, which retains the gravel garden above, as well as the convex wall that drops to the jungle below. I backfilled with rubble, placed the cobbles and spread gravel around them.

This is where we celebrate whatever provides an excuse for celebration. We barbecue on weekends, and we've partied here for anniversaries, posed for graduations, plonked babies down on blankets, and set up tents for grandchildren. Today, however, I've come simply to take a break from the everyday world. It's hot, and I've pulled one of the comfortable Adirondack chairs into the shade. In this heat, I feel as if I'm on holiday. Shall we make it the French Riviera? A beach in Hawaii?

We've always known gardens can be renewing. I wasn't too surprised to read recently that researchers, as researchers are wont to do, have put a name to the notion. The Attention Restoration Theory proposes that certain places have the power to relieve mental fatigue and reboot our brains. The ideal spot has specific qualities. It should create a feeling of immersion. It should represent a change from one's usual surroundings. And it should offer a sense of security. Let's see if the spiral patio is a good candidate for a session of brain restoration!

Immersion is an easy one. The jungle lies below, and the star magnolia's branches reach overhead. To the right, a mock orange wafts its fragrance in my direction, and to the left, a large fig tree creates a dramatic bulk of leaves. I'm thoroughly immersed. I can also tick off change from one's usual surroundings. The patio is some distance from the house and separated from it by flights of steps. This isn't the most convenient arrangement for barbecues, but it does make it feel like a place apart.

Next, we come to security. A neighbour's dog yaps occasionally, half-heartedly, and children laugh in the distance. These are neighbourly sounds. Someone (who deserves a medal) is mowing a lawn with a push mower. As a child, I often fell asleep to this comforting sound as summer days dwindled into night. Intriguingly, there's a fourth factor that researchers call "soft fascination." It refers to experiences that capture our attention in such a subtle way they still leave room for quiet reflection. I'm still mulling this over, so I'll have to get back to you on it.

I can forget the Hawaiian beach. It looks as if I've already landed in the perfect spot, so I'll sit back, close my eyes and wait for mental restoration to begin.

Time passes.

I may have dozed off because I'm becoming aware that late afternoon has slid into early evening. It takes me a moment to collect my wits and wonder with a jolt why the fig tree is moving. Leaves are trembling, branches jiggling. And now I *am* alert because the entire tree has come alive and is rollicking in a fit of laughter. My next, more realistic thought is *bear*. I pry myself up quietly and tiptoe sideways for a better view. The action in the fig tree is too dispersed to be a single bear. Mother and cubs? I tiptoe backward. Fig leaves are large and cast deep shadows. I peer cautiously into the depths and eventually make out, peering down at me, the face of a very small raccoon.

There are few baby animals more appealing than a raccoon kit, and this turns out to be not one but two. How many? Three — no four — all having the time of their lives. This may be the first time they've ever climbed a tree. They wobble with heart-stopping bravado along branches too thin to bear their weight while their mum, securely lodged in a sturdy crook, looks on, apparently unconcerned. I watch until I've had my fill, and then with a satisfied grin and a thoroughly rebooted brain, I head back to the everyday world.

# A Fan of Ferns

I've been looking into the idea of soft fascination. It's no surprise to learn that rhythmic waves, drifting clouds and rustling leaves all have the power to please and calm us. But it turns out certain designs in nature can also reduce our heart rate and deepen our breathing. Surprisingly, these are fractal patterns, shapes that repeat at different scales, like pine cones, snowflakes and ferns.

Ferns are not only fine examples of fractals; they are extremely ancient — dinosaurs came and went while ferns kept calm and carried on. They are deer-resistant opportunists, willing to grow in not much of anything, all of which explains why I love them dearly and why, on this warm afternoon, I'm sitting on the edge of the bridge to soak up their soothing greenness.

My love of these plants is evident throughout the garden, but it doesn't compare with the obsessive collecting craze that struck nineteenth-century Britain when amateur botanists, often women, scrambled about the countryside plucking native species from their habitats. At a time when the recreational activities of respectable housewives were limited to such riveting pursuits as turning their hair into jewelry, pteridomania gave them an excuse to slacken the corsets, hitch up the bloomers and throw themselves enthusiastically at rock faces or into ditches — activities that coincided with early outcroppings of feminism. I wouldn't dream of removing ferns from the wild, but I certainly appreciate the motivations behind such fervour.

I've heard it said that a person knows they're growing old when they start to love a good fern. So be it. Only after we came out west did I begin to appreciate these unpretentious plants. Back east, I didn't particularly admire them, I ate them. In spring, Maritimers traditionally forage for fiddleheads, the spiralled crosiers of ostrich ferns, and sometimes serve them with a startlingly bony fish called gaspereau.

I planted an ostrich fern by the bog garden for old-times' sake, but I won't be importing any gaspereau. I've done my share of picking hairy little bones from between my teeth since my first memorable encounter with the fish. We had just settled into our new Canadian home when a thump on the door one evening revealed a rugged character who stared at me enquiringly.

"Yes?" I stared enquiringly back.

"Gaspereau?" he demanded.

"Gas Pro?" I echoed, completely baffled.

"Gaspereau?" he repeated. Louder. It took time, but eventually I escaped from the conversational gridlock with a load of slippery protein wrapped in newspaper, an advanced education in local gastronomy and the promise of an annual delivery of extremely fresh fish.

The ferns around me all look healthy and intact. Apparently, insects as well as deer avoid them. Nowadays, we humans are warned against eating them in quantity, but Maritimers are not the only ones to enjoy an occasional ferny dish. The First Nations along this coast harvested the rhizomes of bracken fern and ate them baked or roasted. They also used, and probably still use, the liquorice fern for flavouring. From where I'm sitting, I can reach out and pull up a scrap of its stringy rhizome, scratch it clean with my fingernail, nibble it, and feel the tip of my tongue tingle with a sweet and powerful taste of — ooh yes! — liquorice. These tough little plants manage to grow on sheets of rock by lying dormant through the summer, then sprouting afresh as the rains return in fall. Along with moss, they can also drape themselves like furry green garments on the trunks and branches of bigleaf maples.

I tend to associate ferns with damp and shade, but from my perch up here on the bridge, I can see two other native ferns that cope with dry spells — parsley fern and spleenwort. The small curly fronds of parsley fern look fragile, but the impression is misleading. It was one of the first plants to reappear in fields of ash after the eruption of Mount St. Helens in 1980. These are both dainty little things. At the other end of the scale, and directly below me in the bog garden, sprawls the enormous, unruly royal fern. The bog garden has turned into a royal fern garden, and I'm wondering what became of the Japanese iris and the marsh marigold. I know what became of the skunk cabbage. The slugs grazed it to the ground.

Sword ferns are native here and some were already waist-high when we came. They must date back to pre-logging days, or even much, much earlier. Recently, I discovered they may be as old as the oldest trees around them. In the case of the park across the road, that suggests around five hundred years. Old-growth sword ferns? Why aren't we gasping in astonishment? Why aren't we on our knees before them, singing praises and paying scientists to dedicate their lives to the research of such historic plants? A few years ago, I was horrified to read about a devastating dieback of sword ferns in Washington State, the causes and remedy still uncertain. I can't imagine our forests without their green carpets.

But this won't do. I set out today in search of soothing, and I've strayed into the unthinkable. Let's turn this report around, take a few deep breaths and bring ourselves back to the serenity of these ancient fractals.

# Hoses, Skunks and Betty the Pony

I am not in love with hoses. They are ugly tripping hazards and were born uncooperative. Even a century ago, garden writer Karel Čapec warned that rubber hoses had a special predilection for squirting where you least expect it, mowing down perennials, and coiling themselves into knots. Modern materials have failed to reform them.

They are not only willful but big water wasters. We try to be thrifty with the precious liquid, but in the hottest weather, and especially in the veggie patch, we need help that only a hand-held hose or an unaffordable irrigation system provide, which is why I'm out here at 7:30 a.m. watering the beans.

Much as I dislike hoses, they do provide a great excuse for idleness. Standing here directing a spray along the rows, I feel positively useful while doing little more than dreaming on my feet. Back in New Brunswick, where summers could be seriously hot as well as dry, we shared our lives with a plump Welsh pony, Betty, who scoffed at fences, loved company and once ambled into our kitchen where she hoped, I expect, to join us at the table for dinner.

Our water supply came from a shallow well that provided little enough for ourselves, let alone for the garden, and by mid-July the perennials had already packed it in for the year. Our local family of skunks had earlier churned our small lawn into a ploughed field in search of grubs (a task performed on this coast by crows), so I raked the whole thing over and, foolishly, started from scratch with turf. Predictably, a spell of searing heat and drought set in, and day by day, the expensive green carpet shrivelled into startlingly yellow tiles curled up at the edges.

We lived a quiet country life, so whenever a clean car rolled unexpectedly up our bumpy dirt driveway, it was cause for concern. I was horrified one blistering afternoon when a woman in dressy shoes stepped out of a sleek vehicle in a cloud of dust. She introduced herself as Elizabeth from the garden club in town, where she'd heard about our pretty garden and had finally tracked us down on our charming backcountry road. All I could say was,

"Oh my gosh!...I'm afraid...it's not..." but she'd already ducked under the washing line and was frowning in perplexity at the unlovely scene. Having made sure that a version of Kew Gardens wasn't lurking around the corner she decided, after a long pause and with admirable aplomb, to make the best of an impossible situation. She crunched across the cornflake turf and zeroed in on a speck of colour, the indestructible rose campion, still upright at the back of a deep bed of sorrowful leaves.

Betty, meanwhile, spying unexpected company and thrilled by the prospect of a friendly nuzzle, had pushed over her fence and had trotted up from her paddock to join us. She was rapidly approaching our visitor from behind when I spotted impending disaster and yelled, "No, Betty, NO! Get out! Get OUT!" Elizabeth spun round, met Betty nose to nose, let out a shriek, glared at me in horror and promptly took her leave. The whole episode couldn't have been more embarrassing. Or so I thought. I discovered later that Elizabeth normally used her name's diminutive, which was — of course it was — Betty.

# The World of Wow!

Writers who turn a sentence so adroitly they make me laugh aloud, painters who bring scenes to life with a dab of contrasting colour, composers who know when silence is more telling than a sound — their flair amazes me. I have friends who could toss a bunch of cushions into a shipping container and make it feel like home and a grandson who cooks up five-star meals from random leftovers. My granddaughters could drape themselves in bath towels and look like fashion plates.

They certainly haven't caught their sense of style from me. I probably harbour a cultural predisposition for plain living, but that doesn't explain why my clothes verge on dowdy, why I feel that all's well in the wardrobe department if everything matches, preferably in beige. I shy away from anything remotely impractical. Fancy fingernails or flowing hair are non-starters, and I don't do well with accessories. Scarves entangle me. Buckles, belts and bangles are downright dangerous. A daring move on a dance floor turned my first — and only — strapless gown into a topless one. A handsome but slippery skirt at a Scottish New Year's ball popped a button and deserted me in the middle of an eightsome reel. No wonder I choose dependable gear for my travels — roomy, amenable outfits willing to stay put and without a hint of potentially lethal attachments. My favourite is a soil-stained, paint-splattered jumpsuit with stretchy knees.

At this point, I'm wondering if my train of thought has jumped the tracks. Am I confusing plain living with plain laziness? Maybe it's time to reform, and inspired by the panache of my favourite globetrotting writers, make an effort to exhibit more self-assurance in my travel wear. Maybe it's time to throw off the baggy pants and the oversized sweater, slip my feet into something fancier than sneakers, indulge in a creative manicure, throw on a splendid purple shawl of confidence and plonk a hat of authority on my head — the kind of hat that makes a statement.

Let's say I'm striding across the deck as if it were a catwalk. Let's say I'm setting out with an important visitor to inspect the garden. Let's say that visitor is you. So far so good, but the moment I step off the deck, I'm in trouble. I stumble down the steps and my spanking new heels sink into the gravel path. I recover my poise, but the shawl is sliding off my shoulders, and I'm starting to wonder if shawls are remotely fashionable these days. Is purple passé? Were the sparkly fingernails a big mistake? And the hat? I haven't a clue what kind of statement I want to make. So, if you wouldn't mind waiting for a moment, I'll review the headgear of my literary mentors and try some on for size. Paul Theroux wore a style appropriately called Traveler purchased from St. James's Street, London. Not an option on my budget. How about a jaunty bandana? Too youthful. Ball cap? Too sporty. Cowboy buckaroo — for a vegetarian? Head scarf? Too Queen-E-at-Balmoral.

That's it. I'm done already! One paragraph and I've already had enough of makeovers, so I'll return to the house, ditch the shoes and the shawl, dig out my comfy oatmeal cardigan and don my good old reliable sun hat, the one that makes me look like Paddington Bear.

I'm beginning to understand why gardening works for me. All I have to do out here is the practical stuff, the grunt work, the shovelling and raking, the planting and weeding. I kick-start a process, I put in the hours, then I step back and wait.

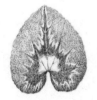  

I don't have to design the leaves of a cyclamen. I don't have to compose the song of a wren or dream up the electric blue of a

Steller's jay. I can plant a sensibly green tree, stand back and marvel as autumn turns it into a towering dazzle of red. A few years of slog, a few moments of awareness, and I too become part of this wonderful world of wow.

# Pondering the Veggies

*I set out to harvest zucchinis but have been waylaid by an unexpected beauty.* The golden, pink and red stems of the rainbow chard are so striking, I'm tempted to arrange some in a glass jug. I don't usually think of the veggie garden as a thing of beauty. Yet here it is, glistening in the early morning sunlight, full of verve and every bit as lovely, in an orderly kind of way, as any flower bed.

The slender leeks are all toeing the line, and although the kale has toppled off course, its puckered foliage is handsomely textured. The rhubarb leaves are, of course, even more dramatic. The zucchinis, with their big yellow trumpet flowers, are almost as decorative as the chard and are doing what happy zucchinis do best — creating a glut. Skip a day's harvesting, and their finger-sized fruits transform into swollen sausages, into blimps, into great green porkers — momma sows snoozing in the shade of their prickly leaves while suckling litters of cute courgettes.

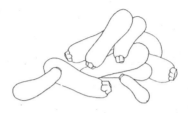

The tomatoes, which I never got round to staking adequately, have flopped into unruly mounds, well-sampled by the deer. Even *they* look decorative this morning, which reminds me that in Europe, they were grown originally as ornamentals. The fruit was first considered toxic, then an aphrodisiac, and even into the twentieth century it was still thought more prudent to cook these suspicious "love apples" with spices and vinegar. Prepared this way, they proved tasty as well as safe — and lo! — tomato ketchup was born. After that, it didn't take long for the world to agree that this once-dodgy crop had been created specifically for the mass production of sauces, soups, pizzas and baked beans.

Some parts of the world were slower to catch on to the tomato craze than others, and I suspect Scotland was slower than most. My grandfather thought of them as fruit, sprinkled segments with sugar and served them with a spoon. I don't know if this was a widespread Scottish custom or a personal eccentricity. He was, after all, the one who taught me to shake pepper on strawberries, a delicious combination that might even rescue those out-of-season lumps on sale in supermarkets. Although Grandad was botanically correct in his claim that tomatoes were fruits, the U.S. Supreme Court disagreed. In 1887, the country placed a duty on vegetables, and when tomato growers objected to the inclusion of their product, a judge ruled in favour of the tax declaring tomatoes were "a principal part of the repast and not a dessert."

Moving on from the tomatoes, I come to the parsnips. All three of them. I love roasted parsnip — so earthy, so autumnal — but last year, after yet another dismal crop, I swore off growing them. This spring, however, I discovered an undated seed packet with a tiny pinch still left in the corner. To my surprise, four germinated. One vanished. For advice on parsnip growing, I should turn to Terry, queen of everything vegetable, whose parsnips remind me of the Russian folk tale of a farmer's turnip so mighty its unearthing required the efforts of an entire family plus neighbours, dog, cat and, finally, mouse.

I pick a stem from a clump of chives and chew on it as I ponder Terry's gardening prowess. Her veggie gluts are far more spectacular than anything we produce. I grow veggies; she grows VEGGIES. Our leeks are blades of grass alongside her stout columns. By autumn, when their huge leaves die away, her hefty and unblemished butternut squash would win ribbons at any fall fair. I'm convinced this bounty is due to her skill as a scavenger. A little light dumpster diving often yields splendid selections of plant pots and once produced a wrought iron fence that serves as fine trellis-work for clematis. She turns driftwood into garden furniture, creates plant props from the wire of abandoned political signs, and turns old pantyhose into stretchy plant ties. She even fashions her old black tights — along with foraged feathers — into realistically dead crows. These fakes, placed upside down on the garage roof, effectively protect her nesting birds from the real marauders. Her ultimate foraging success, however, is seaweed, a magical substance containing not only the big three — nitrogen, phosphorus and potassium — but scores of trace elements with a few growth hormones thrown in. No wonder it's been used to boost crops for at least 2,000 years. My first and last attempt to follow my friend's admirable example ended with an abundance of angry shore life in the car trunk and a surprisingly meagre haul of fertilizer in the garden.

I do better with pole beans than with parsnips. A friend recommended the variety Fortex, which sounds more like a foreign exchange market than a bean, but the crops have been impressive. As I picked some of these long tender pods yesterday, I noticed every stem twined around the canes in the same direction. Anticlockwise, as seen from above. I was curious to know if all plants rotate that way and if they alter course in the southern hemisphere. It turns out that hemispheres have as little effect on twining stems as they do on water swirling down plugholes. Different plants, however, spiral in different directions. Hops, for instance, choose clockwise. Some species of wisteria are right-handed and some are lefties, while cucumber tendrils are ambidextrous.

Next, I wondered if snail shells also turn one way. They do — clockwise from the inside out — although rare individuals spiral in reverse. I'll never look at a snail again without checking its orientation. One of these shells is not like the others.

# The Long Arm of Friendship

I greet many old friends as I roam through the garden: *Julie's rhubarb, Joan's hellebore, Audrey's persicaria, Terry's Michaelmas daisy.* I'm sure any well-established plot gathers many such names.

Julie was a colleague from way back who gave me a chunk of the rhubarb that now flourishes mightily at the foot of the veggie plot. Last spring, I donated a hefty crown to our new neighbours' garden where, with a little luck, it may morph into Elspeth's rhubarb. Julie also presented me with a pathetically lopsided Japanese maple she'd rescued from a nursery dump. It now lives by the gravel garden, looking every bit as splendid and symmetrical as an expensive, garden-centre version growing nearby.

In the shady bed, Joan's hellebores are also doing well. Joan loved these Lenten roses as much as I do, but she lived in Saskatoon, where winters are too severe for them. When she visited us, we'd browse the garden centres on hellebore-hunting expeditions, and she'd always end up giving me one. In the same bed is Kate's rhododendron, a replacement for his old man, 'Sir Charles Lemon', who succumbed suddenly a few years ago. Our thoughtful daughter knew how upset I was, and she scoured British Columbia's garden centres until she found his successor.

A very special plant grows along the railing of the deck. Judy's honeysuckle began its long journey from a nursery in Ontario almost fifty years ago. It travelled by rail, bare root but carefully packaged, to our garden in New Brunswick, where it covered an unsightly stump and was much loved by hummingbirds. After Judy arrived from the States to live nearby, I gave her a rooted slip of the plant. When Ray and I moved west, I kept in touch with my friend by mail, and when she finally visited us here, she brought a piece of this lovely vine with her. Judy died some years ago, and the heartbreak was hard to bear, but her honeysuckle lives on, still loved by hummingbirds, and it remains, in some very slight way, a comfort.

In these reports, when I mention a hummingbird called Alf, a ladylike clematis called Hagley or a rowdy rhododendron called Vulcan, you must have noticed I often regard plants and animals as friends in their own right. Biologists rightly shudder at the thought of endowing creatures with

human characteristics, let alone turning plants into people. All I can do is apologize to the scientifically minded and blame Beatrix Potter. I've already gone too far down this road to back up now, and besides, it's a road many have travelled before me. The Greeks were particularly fond of transforming trees into gods or nymphs and vice versa. More recently, tree-like Ents inhabit J.R.R. Tolkien's Middle-earth, while Steve and Ed, the evil trees in *Shrek*, converse in cockney accents. Europeans usually regard trees as the good guys, but only the ignorant or foolhardy would dare to treat a rowan or an oak with disrespect. Around the world, palm nuts, manioc and mandrake roots have all populated our imaginations.

Here on the Pacific Coast, a First Nations' story tells of Pitch, an invaluable character who helps out with caulking canoes, sealing containers, fuelling torches and healing wounds. Pitch always rose early to go fishing in the cool of morning, but one day he set out too late, and the warm sun melted him into a puddle. Douglas fir saw what happened, rushed over and poured the useful gluey substance over himself. Grand fir was hot on his heels and scraped up the rest so, by the time arbutus arrived on the scene, it was all gone. Embellished by a good storyteller, this simple tale would have far more staying power than any lecture on the resin contents of the local trees.

I don't pretend that Hagley-the-clematis or Vulcan-the-rhododendron have any educational value, but they do populate this place with their strong personalities. We inherited many such striking plants from the previous owners, whom we never met.

I've always wanted to let them know how much their enthusiastic presence lingers here.

Dear previous owners,

You'll be surprised to hear from me after all this time, but I'd like to thank you for the intriguing variety of plants you passed on to us.

You probably remember your magnolia, Star. She's a little arthritic now but grows lovelier by the year. Your rhododendron, Augustus, has also lived on to become part of our lives as he must have been of yours. A few of your charges have grown so tall you'd hardly recognize them. Your Japanese umbrella pine, Brolly, has broadened out from a spindly teen to a fine upstanding fellow.

How happy we've all been here! I hope you're enjoying your new garden, wherever it may be, as much as we're enjoying the gifts of your old one.

In friendship,

Elspeth Bradbury

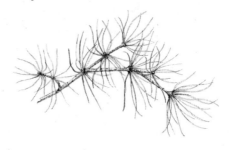

# New Eyes

I was watering a drought-stricken camellia yesterday when a female hummingbird flew daringly close to the sparkling arc of spray. I held the hose nozzle steadily for fear of drenching her, although I know a hummingbird in flight can shake off raindrops as efficiently as a shaggy dog. She grew bolder with each approach. Was she drinking? Bathing? Playing? Possibly all three because she suddenly flattened herself against the dripping surface of a large camellia leaf, loosed her grip and — whee! — slid all the way down. She seemed delighted with this trick and repeated it on a droopy-wet fern frond before zooming off to perch and preen nearby.

I witnessed these surprising antics because the hose had anchored me to the spot. If there's one thing my journeys have shown me so far, it's that slowing down and staying put are the best ways to elicit moments of "Oh, a-ha!" Once in April, as I came to a standstill in the jungle, a flock of golden-crowned sparrows enveloped me as if they might land on my shoulders. Another time, a small Douglas squirrel briefly mistook me for a tree. Back in May, I joined the atmospheric festival of insects only because I was sitting quietly on the bench. When I took a moment to admire the glorious buds of a tree peony, I noticed an alligator lizard sunning on a rock below. After I paused for a breather in a raking session, I immediately spotted an elegant black and yellow garter snake, the first I've seen in the garden.

Obviously, I have no need to dash about in search of surprises. Hold steady and the world simply rolls my way, unstoppable and full of revelations. I know this, yet I'm still inclined to buzz about like a bee on a blueberry bush. How can I learn to take my time? Would a camera help me to focus? Photographer Freeman Patterson, a friend from our days in New Brunswick, has always taught that real seeing takes time and involves intellect, emotions and all the senses. A camera sounds like the perfect tool, but a sketchbook would be a better bet for me. One of my heroes, Scottish-American John Muir, almost always carried one. He travelled extensively through North America on foot, was a tireless defender of the natural landscape, and is known in the States as the "Father of the National Parks." Here was a man of action who nevertheless understood the rewards of stillness. When, for instance, he came across a plant he'd never seen before, he'd sit beside it for an hour, for a day, for as long as it took to feel his way into its life, to "discover its nature."

Muir was so eager to pay attention to the world that he sometimes attempted to see it from a different angle. To appreciate the grandeur of a mountain scene, he might bend over to view it upside down. Eccentric, maybe, but worth a try? Once, during a Sierra storm, he climbed to the top of a Douglas fir and rode the tree for hours, thrilled by its motion, the roar of the wind and the fragrance of the forest streaming by. He later described with breathless enthusiasm the sight of the treetops below his perch rippling like a field of grain.

As a small child, I used to tuck myself comfortably into the high crotch of a rowan tree, which grew in our front garden, and from my bird's eye view, I'd spy on the world passing underneath. I haven't climbed any trees lately, but from the deck, I have a good view of the garden below. Who knows what I'd see if I spent more time leaning quietly on the rail and gazing *down* at this familiar ground?

I can't remember when I first read Laurie Lee's *Cider with Rosie*, but his description of a world seen from another perspective — from knee level — has stayed with me. As a toddler, he'd been dumped (until his doting sisters rescued him) in long grass that towered over his head. Each blade of grass was "tattooed with tiger-skins of sunlight. It was knife-edged, dark and a wicked green, thick as a forest and alive with grasshoppers that chirped and chattered and leapt through the air like monkeys."

Today, on the patio, I feel almost as bewildered as the young Laurie Lee. I've brought a blanket and Dervla Murphy's *Muddling Through in Madagascar*, but after reading the same paragraph three times, I put the book down. This extraordinary traveller deserves my full attention. The warm gravel moulds comfortably to my back. I relax and stare up. Across an aerial corridor, between the cedar and the hemlock, a spider has slung a perfectly constructed web. Three silken guy lines catch the sunlight. The spider herself, a dark dot in the centre of the gently ballooning disc, has performed astonishing feats of abseiling to cast her net so cleverly at such a height. As I gaze, web and spider vanish, extinguished by the shift of the sun's trajectory. I lie, thinking about the words of Marcel Proust, "The real voyage of discovery consists not in seeking new landscapes, but in having new eyes."

The longer I stare up, the more disoriented I become. Sunlight splashes and splinters through foliage that begins to look utterly unfamiliar and exotic. The trees around me reach dizzying heights — or depths? They enclose a ragged circle of immaculate sky, which, through my half-closed eyes, begins to resemble a pool of deep water. A small bird (a minnow?) darts across the blue. The surface begins to waver. Too much glare. The blanket is rumpled. I gather it up, retrieve my book and slowly, slowly make my way back to the house.

# Garden Oddballs

In the gravel garden, the cyclamen flowers have popped up despite the parched soil and heat of August. The cyclamen leaves won't arrive on the scene until fall when their unique patterns will decorate the ground all winter. I'd grow these plants for that alone, but in the meantime, there's the bonus of these tiny flowers. Strangely reflexed and twisted, they look as if their ears have blown back in astonishment as if they can hardly believe they've come into the world at such an inauspicious time of year.

A few of their petals have dropped already, and something peculiar is happening. Just below the developing seed capsules, stems have started to curl. Others have already coiled themselves all the way down and are "planting" their capsules in the ground, where they'll stay protected in spirals as tightly wound as liquorice wheels. Wouldn't you love to see this magical performance recorded in time-lapse photography? The ingenious process takes place on an equally unusual platform. The delicate pointed flower buds emerge from rock-hard tubers that lie near the surface of the soil and resemble small dry cowpats. They don't look tempting, but a common name, sowbread, suggests they appeal to pigs.

Several bumblebees, as big as the flowers themselves, are working the patch over. It's a tricky upside-down business for them with their fully loaded pollen sacks. Pollen is a valuable by-product of their search for nectar. Using their front legs, they comb it off their furry bodies and then return to their nests with this precious baby food packed into specially constructed pouches on their hind legs. I read recently a negative charge on certain flowers attracts a positive charge on the bees themselves, so the pollen not only rubs off on the insects but obligingly jumps right onto them.

Most of the bumblebees I'm watching have gathered yellow pollen from the cyclamen, but one of them is carting around a bright orange cargo that may have come from a different fall-flowering plant, one that grows under the elm tree in the driveway bed. People wonder why our crocuses are flowering there at this time of year. There *are* such things as fall-flowering crocuses — their dried stamens are the valuable spice, saffron — but these crocus look-alikes are colchicums, a different plant altogether. The lilac chalices with their bright orange centres arrive, like the cyclamen flowers, leafless, which explains a common name, naked ladies. Their green garb won't appear until spring when their big, floppy foliage will feed the corms and disappear long before the next floral display begins. They are the source of colchicine, a powerful medication that's also used to manipulate the genes of plants to produce double flowers and larger, hardier or faster-growing varieties as well as anomalies such as seedless watermelons. Unexpectedly, for a plant that can be lethal to humans, our emerging flowers have attracted slugs. One can only hope colchicine doesn't produce bigger, hardier and faster-growing gastropods.

Down in the jungle, doll's eyes are another oddity. Their weird berries stick out on bright red stalks and really do resemble white eyeballs dotted with small, black pupils. Awesome!

Back in May, when I was raving about my beloved woodland peonies, I promised to describe their seed heads later in the year. Well, here we are. These oddball structures are now at their most eye-catching, and I've come to enjoy them in the shady bed.

The fat pods, curving like the padded horns of a jester's cap, are grouped in sets of five but, strangely, also come in threes or fours. They start out as small green bananas that dry out over summer and split along their upper seams to reveal not pasty flesh but two ranks of bright red seeds. By now, the splits have widened, and the pods are flattening into grinning mouths crammed with crimson molars. Set among them, as plump and glossy as blue-black pearls, are a few bigger versions that seem to shoulder out their smaller kin. You'd think these were bullies — cuckoos in the nest — but no! These are the real things, the fertile seeds. If I plant them right away, they'll probably take two years to appear above-ground, and a few more years to produce the next generation of seeds. They are well worth the wait.

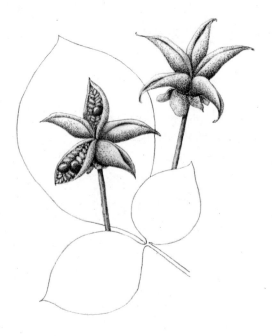

# How the Other Half Lives

I'm expecting visitors tomorrow, so there's no idle wandering for me today. I'm watering the wilted, trimming the untidy, weeding the unwanted and propping up the faint of heart. Gardening at times can feel a lot like trying to wrangle a reluctant family into a group photo. "Back off, Laurel. Lean in, Daphne. For heaven's sake, all of you, smile!" The uncles are grumpy, the teens are sulky and the kids are going bananas. I can plead for a little cooperation, but I know that the perfectly posed picture, frozen for posterity, is never going to happen — not in this garden anyway.

To support the flopping stems of a bellflower, I stab a cane into the ground. The roots are surprisingly dense. The cane snaps off and, in the pause that follows, it occurs to me that while I'm attempting to persuade unruly plants to behave themselves above ground, I know very little of what's going on below the surface. Is everybody playing nice down there?

When I began my garden journeys, I hoped, a tad ambitiously, to see the world, but despite my best efforts, I'm seeing only half of it. Not even that. Recently, I came across an eye-opening online site created by researchers at Wageningen University in the Netherlands, showing a vast collection of painstakingly excavated root systems drawn to scale. The underground portion of most species, from Douglas fir to dandelion, dwarfs the overground portion by sheer bulk or by an astonishing width or depth.

Thanks to the work of other dedicated researchers, we now know there's much more going on down there than we once imagined. Roots aren't just sucking up water, they're leading busy social lives. Fungal networks are linking forest trees into communities that may be just about as helpful, gossipy or selective as their human counterparts. Now, when I walk in the old-growth park across the road, I try to imagine the exchanges going on beneath my feet.

I caught a revealing glimpse of this underground world when I converted the pond into the gravel garden. When I stripped away the old liner, the sand directly below the sheeting was a solid mat of roots, some as fine as thread, others as tough as rope, and all so tightly intertwined it was impossible to trace them back to their owners. For decades they'd been burrowing down there, taking advantage of the cool moist conditions. Exposing this unexpected network felt strangely intrusive, and I covered it up as quickly as I could.

After all this rooty reflection, I've now given up on the bellflower, and I'm off to pull salal suckers from the path beside one of the large cedars. Most plants refuse to live contentedly beside a tree as hungry, thirsty and shady as a cedar, but salal thrives here. Perhaps their roots are negotiating some kind of secret deal through fungal go-betweens.

Fungi, it seems, can be choosey. Those that consort with these western redcedars also prefer the company of maple and yew. Those that fancy birch also like to buddy up with Douglas fir. In an old-growth forest like the one across the road, our native plants have been hanging out together for thousands of years, so they've worked out some long-term relationships by now. Still, I can't help wondering if the plants in this garden have been together long enough to create any kind of society. Will they ever settle happily into a cohesive multicultural community? How do the old timers react when I introduce, for instance, a maple from Japan? A sourwood from the Southern U.S.? Will the western redcedar and its fungal friends take to the hedge of eastern cedar? And what part do the smaller plants play? Is the native ginger more socially acceptable than ginger from the Old World? Who's in cahoots?

Who's in competition? Are squabbles breaking out? Does the rhubarb love the squash?

So many questions, so few answers, and I'm fine with that. As Henry James wrote, "I can wish the traveller no better fortune than to stroll forth in the early evening with as large a reserve of ignorance as my own."

# A Blizzard of Moths and A Blood-Red Sun

Even the media took note. "Metro Vancouver overrun. Trees under attack. Watch out Vancouver — the moths are coming." Every decade or so, the population of hemlock looper moths builds up in this part of the world. We don't know how climate change will affect this pattern in the future, but a few years ago, the outbreak was dramatic. It began with insubstantial flickers of reflected light in the dusk. Then, as darkness deepened, more and more insects gathered. By the third night, the swarms were so dense, I did feel a momentary tremor of unease despite the headlines' belated reassurances. *Moth influx no cause for panic. No reason to bug out.* This year, the invasion is less dramatic, but Hitchcock's 1963 movie *The Birds* still comes to mind this evening as I watch the flutter of wings around the porch light.

The moths are also drawn to our kitchen window, where, exhausted, stunned or entranced, they flatten themselves against the glass. An intimate view of their underwings shows them to be primly pretty, as delicate as tissue paper, demurely beige or silver-grey and embroidered in dainty scallops — far from menacing. The males have elaborate feathery antennae that equip them to detect scent signals from the females.

I wonder, as many have wondered before, why these nocturnal creatures are cursed with a craving for light, a compulsion so strong they seem in the grip of a powerful drug or caught up in a crazy cult of adoration. Nobody knows for sure why moths dash themselves against street lamps or singe their wings in campfires, but ideas abound. One suggests that the males confuse heat and light with qualities of the female pheromones. An ingenious older theory proposes that their actions are indeed lunatic — that moths use the moon for navigation and, by lining it up at a constant angle to their flight, can keep themselves on a straight course. If, however, they focus on a street light by mistake and keep moving at a constant angle to its glow, the flight path circles around until the hapless creature blunders into the lamp itself. I like this explanation, but I gather it's out of favour with those in the know.

The large paper globe hanging over our kitchen table must draw the insects to this particular window. With the click of the light switch, I can extinguish their fake moon or release them from the charismatic hold of their idol. One by one they depart until only the stunned or the true believers remain, and by morning they too are gone, some to join the litter of papery wings that collect in the corners of the deck.

Summer evenings of fluttery moths have been less unnerving in recent years than mornings of smoky skies, evidence of wildfires raging in the province. Dawns have arrived with an orange cast and the malevolent glare of a blood-red sun. A sullen grey has layered the nearby landscape into the flats of a sombre stage set, and an eerie stillness has settled over the garden. Even the birds have avoided strenuous outdoor exercise. On such days, we've missed the inconstant sky, the cumulus clouds piling up like soft meringue against the North Shore Mountains and the fleeting shell-pink glow of reflected sunsets.

With the sudden change from transparent sunshine to the gloom of deadened light, a sense of unreality infiltrates the house, and we go about our lives as if we were role-playing. The pervasive smoky smell reminds us of our student days in England's industrial North, when thousands of chimneys belched out a smog of coal smoke, which soiled our clothes, blackened buildings and blocked the sunlight for days at a time.

Since prehistory, we've wondered why light appears to attract moths, and finally, we're close to solving the mystery. An international team of researchers using high-speed infrared video discovered that moths fly with their backs toward light. Because the night sky glows more brightly than the ground, this allows the insects to maintain a level flight path. However, if they come across an artificial light source and turn their backs on it by mistake, they lose their sense of up and down. Confused, they begin to orbit and may eventually stall or flip over completely.

# Nurturing the Gardener's Inner Child

*L*ook carefully as we walk through the jungle, and you may spot a small figure crouched among the ferns. An important job for a troll is to guard a bridge, and this particular fellow, though no larger than a turnip, carries out his responsibility dutifully. For decades, he has kept an eye on the crossing that spans the creek, and he decamps from his post only when friendly children feel he needs a break from this arduous task. Trolls have dubious reputations, but despite his belligerent expression, our small resident seems benevolent enough. Possibly he enjoys his colourful toenails, which may owe something to Ray's skill with oil paints. However, on that subject, as on all others, Troll retains a stony silence.

Troll's presence here puts me in mind of garden styles that are often inventions of the male mind. I think of them as folk gardens. We saw plenty of them in Atlantic Canada, but I seldom see them

here on the West Coast. Perhaps they've become endangered species. Perhaps in these sophisticated times, we've grown too serious-minded or, heaven forbid, too terribly tasteful for such fun.

A folk garden is easy to spot because the open-hearted creator loves to share his yard, and usually his sense of humour, with passersby. He may start out with nothing more than a garden gnome and a spinning sunflower picked up at the local hardware store. They brighten up the front yard, so he adds a fibreglass frog and a pair of pink flamingos. The true folk gardener, however, is born only when he starts to set his purchased collection in a homemade landscape. He whitewashes rocks to line the driveway, pipes in a fancy fountain and clips a bush into the shape of a duck. If he lives in a rural area, he rescues an obsolete plough from the barn and shows it off along with shiny, cast-off hubcaps. He cuts tractor tires into zigzags like giant radishes to serve as raised beds for cheerful annuals. For additional planters, he co-opts old wheelbarrows, coal scuttles or a bathtub. If he lives by the sea, he plants up a derelict dinghy and edges a beach-pebble path with floats and clam shells.

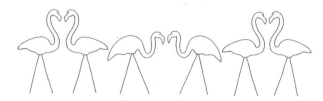

The handyman gardener adds a few tongue-in-cheek signs to amuse the neighbours, and his craftsmanship grows more ambitious. Miniature windmills and gulls with revolving wings come whirling off his production line. He hies himself off to the shed to dig out plywood offcuts, which he jigsaws into whimsical creatures of his own design — cats, rabbits, deer and his magnum opus, a herd of Holstein cattle.

Gardens imbued with a spirit of play are nothing new. For centuries, crowing roosters, galloping horses and flapping herons have swivelled on weather vanes. Ingenious sundials have told us more about the love of gadgetry than the time of day. The fascination with outdoor ornaments and clever contrivances peaked in the gardens of the Italian Renaissance when the rich and ambitious vied to create impressive entertainment. They indulged their fancies in abundant statuary recalling stories of romance and heroism. With deep pockets and brilliant engineering, they persuaded water to gush in spectacular fountains, cascade down stairways, spout from the mouths of monsters and even play organ music. A watery dining table floated dishes past rows of seated guests. Hidden ducts splashed unsuspecting visitors or jetted frivolously up the skirts of promenading ladies. All good fun, no doubt, though history fails to record how the dripping victims felt about such practical jokes.

It's a big jump from the extravagance of the Villas d'Este or Aldobrandini to our present garden in suburban Vancouver, but some of the features aren't 9,000 km or five centuries apart. We don't have an alley of 100 fountains, but we do have Fish Face, a properly weird gargoyle created by our friend Helen, a ceramic artist from Horseshoe Bay. Fish Face trickles water into a magnificent slipware saucer ($10 many years ago from Ikea) that overflows into a pebble bed where it collects in an old laundry sink and is pumped into a recycled toilet tank hidden beneath the deck. Clever stuff! Proud of this cunning plumbing, we lined up two very small grandchildren to surprise them with the show. We should have realized Fish Face was mounted at precisely their eye level. When we flicked on the hidden switch and water spewed suddenly from the ceramic lips, they fled screaming in horror and had to be comforted with ice cream, a reaction similar, I imagine, to that of Italian women coping with drenched petticoats.

# Stormy Weather

Overnight, the wind swept away September's hesitancy and landed us in full-blown fall. Elm leaves swirl in the driveway. Bigleaf maple leaves hurtle across the road and snag on the rose bushes, where they flutter like tattered, brown paper bags. Overhead, the wind is a high-pitched thrum, and a deeper-throated roar from the forest warns this is no time to visit the park. Trees burdened with wet foliage can snap like twigs, and on saturated soils, shallow rooted giants can topple and heave their massive root plates clear out of the ground.

Even the garden is no place to loiter when trees are creaking and debris is flying. I cancel today's journey and retreat to the porch, where I watch in safety as the trees respond to the blustery onslaughts. Each invents its own choreography. Cedar boughs whirl in a frenzy. Magnolia branches jounce, distraught. Douglas firs are more restrained, but when the wind dies down, it will be *their* branches littering the roadways. In the distance, tall trunks lean and sway.

In the Shetland Islands, the wind blew with an unobstructed force that felt solid. Here, it arrives in turbulent blasts that shift up or down or sideways so that even a Shetlander would be hard-pressed to distinguish between an east-northeaster and a west-southwester. Our flag (we should have taken it down yesterday) flaps away from the house, whips back and twirls itself clammily around the pole. Down here, I cower as another wet salvo comes stinging toward me.

My imaginary garden, the one sitting in the back of my mind, smiling prettily with never a leaf out of place, has decamped in a hurry. The brains of most gardeners cling stubbornly to such visions of orderly perfection despite overwhelming evidence that we're delusional. Every garden visitor has heard our mournful cries. If only you had seen it last week, last month, last year, before the drought, before the frost, before the storm. And next year, all will be perfect, right? My real garden is, as a French Prime Minister with an astonishing lack of tact once described Argentina, "A place with a wonderful future — and always will be." Rare indeed is the gardener who harbours no illusions of control, who acknowledges with grace that the vagaries of weather will always confound us. My friend Judy was one of the blessed few. She greeted any small gardening success with astonishment and gratitude, thrilled if a rose bush bloomed through summer and just as thrilled if it didn't freeze to death in winter. Oh, Judy, I miss you!

Meanwhile, this storm confines me to the porch and is hell-bent on mayhem. Or is it? Wasn't I bemoaning the stifling temperatures a month ago? Wasn't I pleading for rain a few weeks ago? Rough weather plays a role in any interesting journey. Every well-worn traveller expects to cross paths with bouts of feverish heat or with glacial cold and a storm or two. Today's windy clamour is neither a bellow of anger nor a howl of despair. It's only the sound of the seasons cranking over as they should. By now, we can hardly remember the time of blossoms and whistling robins. The berry-picking season is long past, and we're well into the moon of shaking leaves. Trees are transferring a harvest of energy into their root cellars for safekeeping. In the woods, the fallen are making room for newcomers and will nurse and nurture them into the future.

Storms and forests, storms and gardens — these are old, old stories. In 1962, Typhoon Freda felled three thousand trees in Vancouver's Stanley Park. In 2006, the wind toppled its trees like dominoes. The damage seemed irreparable. Some of England's most famous gardens, established for centuries, were unrecognizable after a storm in 1987 flattened fifteen million trees, including six of the ancient oaks that gave the town of Sevenoaks its name. And afterwards? New vistas opened. Opportunities arose. Little by little, forests recovered, renewed. Gardens were reimagined and remade, as gardens always have been. Tomorrow, the commotion will die down. Tomorrow, the squirrels and the hummingbirds will emerge from their hideaways. Tomorrow, I'll find a winter coat, and we'll all get back to work.

# Say the Names

Today I've made an itinerary. I'll start with a few circuits of the Gravel Garden, where I'll check on the Turtle Pond, then I'll make my way along the Shady Path to the Spiral Patio and down through the Jungle to the Bench...

At this point, it occurs to me that my brain is adding capital letters to all these names. I grew up steeped in the work of A.A. Milne and the unforgettable illustrations of E.H. Shepard. The Hundred Acre Wood, Owl's Tree and Eeyore's House (his gloomy place, rather boggy and sad) were as familiar to me as my own neighbourhood. No wonder this lot, our Third of an Acre Wood, is riddled with our own place names. We didn't create them deliberately. They simply came about as we worked our way around the place. If Ray wanted to tell me where he'd left the wheelbarrow, he might say it's on the Big Rock and I'd know exactly where to find it.

These names are handy aids to orientation, and they're certainly more fun than GPS coordinates, but they also evoke memories

that tie us to our history on this piece of land. We're still inclined to call the Gravel Garden the Pond, and the extra parking space alongside the Driveway is still the Truck Park, although our trusty six-cylinder workhorse is long gone, its bodywork rusted out by road salt from the east coast and by humid winters here on the "wet" coast.

Place names can have staying power, but this hasn't always been the case in British Columbia, where colonialism wiped out many of them. Local languages would have been thick with useful or historical references to villages and campsites as well as resource locations or vantage points such as fishing spots or mountain peaks. Settlers quickly installed new names, but these seldom grew out of the land itself or bore any relationship to it. I think of them as parachute appellations — Victoria, New Westminster, Prince George, Mount Garibaldi.

The modern name of our local village, Horseshoe Bay, while somewhat descriptive, fails to conjure up the memorable image of its original name Ch'axáý, which is said to mimic the sizzling sound of an inlet once alive with spawning herring. Even closer to home, a lighthouse, built in 1874 and replaced in 1912, stands at the tip of our neighbouring park where Burrard Inlet pivots into Howe Sound. The headland, now known as Point Atkinson, was named, like many other geographical features on this coast, by Captain Vancouver of the British Navy in honour of a colleague. The First Nations' name, pronounced approximately Skay-wit-sut, means turning point and is far more appropriate for a spot that has always been a vital landmark for marine navigation.

Spoken names fix places in our brains. Accumulated over centuries of living with the land, they create a common language and in turn, a sense of community. When useful, spiritual, sad or funny place names are lost, we lose layers of useful, spiritual, sad or funny human history, and all our lives are poorer for it. I believe we also lose a sense of belonging — an attachment to place that may be almost as important to our well-being as an attachment to people.

Canadian poet Al Purdy understood the power of place names and expressed it in his poem "Say the Names." I wish our names for this garden would "ride the wind" like his "Spillimacheen, Nahanni, Illecillewaet and Kleena Kleene." We seem to be stuck with our prosaic Driveway, Bench and Bridge, and I sometimes wonder if this plot of land was ever endowed with more poetic titles. In this reflective frame of mind, I murmur to myself, "say the names say the names and listen to yourself an echo in the mountains Tulameen…" I can't remember the rest, but I know its rhythms will stay with me for the rest of my journey today.

# Parsnips and Potatoes

With Thanksgiving dinner in mind, I came to the veggie patch this morning and finally lifted the three promising parsnips. They came up easily. Far too easily because the things that dangled from bunches of greenery in my hands were more turnip than parsnip, nubs as round as tennis balls. The bowl of potatoes at my feet is adequate compensation for the lack of parsnip. I didn't dig these ones from the rows we harvested earlier. This plant was a volunteer. It grew a great sprawling top that has now contributed enough potatoes for our Thanksgiving dinner and beyond. It seems appropriate that, growing unbidden, it stirs in me a deep sense of gratitude.

When I'm out here in the garden, I sometimes feel as if I have a connection with the plants that goes beyond familiarity. Do I sometimes think that it's reciprocal? Do I believe plants can be tuned in to human emotions? If I talk encouragingly to the beans, do I expect them to be more productive? Not really. If I lean against

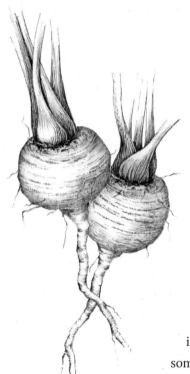

a tree trunk in a friendly way, is it because I think the tree will wrap its branches around me in a loving hug? No, but I do it anyway.

Travel writer Robert Macfarlane recounts being struck forcefully by the realization that nature was immune to his emotions when he travelled to the north of Scotland. In his book *The Wild Places*, he tells how, marooned on a mountaintop, he found, to his consternation, "here there was no question of relation." It wasn't a sense of hostility that disturbed him but nature's complete indifference. I've experienced this sort of loneliness myself, and I don't have to camp on the summit of Ben Hope to rediscover it. Yet there's no doubt the natural world offers something to us in return for our attention. Although it may not love us, it doesn't hate us either, and perhaps this complete, unemotional acceptance consoles us, relieves us of the obligations and complexities inherent in all our human relationships. We are simply, fully part of it.

Of course, vegetables don't expect thanks in return for their bounty. Nevertheless, when Ray and I sit down to our evening meal tonight, we'll be profoundly grateful for the privilege of travelling on this astonishing planet along with the squirrels and cedars, the robins and raccoons, the parsnips and potatoes.

# Questionable Rock-Frog and Blood-Spattered Beard

When Ray heard the patter of tiny claws in the attic, we knew the time had come to call in the roofers. Confirmation came the next morning when a pretty little roof rat joined us as we sat in the porch enjoying the last of the year's warmth. It perched on the corner of the lean-to greenhouse with its long tail dangling and gave us sidelong glances. When we protested, it scampered up the roof and disappeared.

Now I'm standing on the deck, staring up at the new cladding of recycled rubber shingles. However handsome and vermin-proof it may be, I'm still feeling a little sad that the old cedar shakes have gone. On their accommodating surface, a miniature forest of lichens had grown up — a living community quite distinct from anything else in the garden.

I once carried out an unintentional experiment that showed me how much life can exist in such miniature ecosystems. When the children were small, I was, as usual, trying to think of original Christmas presents to give to friends, and I hit on the idea of planting bottle gardens. We collected mosses and lichens from the woods, stuffed them into wide-topped glass jars, added artfully placed twigs and stones, proudly corked our pixie gardens, then wrapped them to await the usual pre-Christmas gathering. The grand reveal was a disaster. Why on earth, our friends wondered unhappily, had we presented them with decaying vegetation and hordes of bottled insects?

I liked the way our rooftop lichens gave the house a well-established look, but apart from sweeping up the debris dislodged by foraging jays, I didn't pay much attention to them. This seems to be their lot in life, and for this very reason, lichenologists led by the Canadian Museum of Nature began a publicity stunt some years ago on behalf of their overlooked and underappreciated subjects. While most of us were glued to our social media feeds, these admirable stalwarts were calculating Canada's lichen biomass (probably the world's greatest) and organizing an online contest to choose Canada's national lichen. They selected seven species out of a possible 2,500 or so and asked the public to pick a winner. Not included in the short list were questionable rock-frog and blood-spattered beard. Devil's matchstick, pencil script and antlered perfume also failed to make the grade. Lichenologists obviously had far too much fun when they named these things. However, if you spend your days gazing at something as easy to miss as a dab of chewing gum on a sidewalk and that grows — flat out — more slowly than your fingernails, I suppose you get your jollies where you can.

With my pale Scottish skin, my personal favourite in the contest would have been the common freckle pelt. The prize, however, went to the star-tipped reindeer, which grows in every province and is an important winter food for caribou. A sound choice.

Unlike killer whales, Siberian tigers or giant redwoods, lichens usually fail to set the human pulse a-racing, which may explain why funding agencies don't rush to splash cash on their research. The 1,800 biologists and other fans who voted during the month-long popularity poll are doubtless passionate and dedicated individuals, willing to scrounge a living and spend their vacations on hands and knees in remote, blackfly-infested locations, peering at rocks through a hand lens. A lichen hunt with one of them is likely, I imagine, to turn into a slither.

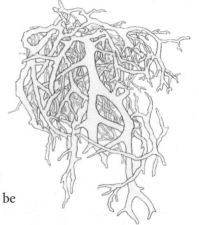

If I turn my back on the house and look into the branches of the star magnolia, I see a fine collection of lichens right there. The tree must be at least fifty years old but even the nearby stewartia, which we planted less than twenty years ago, is prettily sprigged in silvery clusters. I take this as a good sign because lichens don't tolerate poor air quality. These enigmatic crusty things are not a single form of life. We can think of them as fungi that farm algae for their sugars or as algae that have latched onto fungi for security. Although the two have lived as one for eons, some, if separated, can still return to their ancient lives as singles. And it turns out the relationships can be more than two-way. Cyanobacteria and possibly other evolutionary scraps have joined in. These little nonconformists may not shout and leap about, but their living arrangements are stirring stuff for biologists, and even I am well on the way to becoming a lichen fan.

# Unlikely Destinations

Travel writers seem drawn to the unsettling realms that lie well beyond the picture postcards and the tourist brochures. In my role as fellow traveller, I've decided it's time to follow in their footsteps, so I'm on my way to explore, not a shantytown in Calcutta, nor a back alley of shady repute in Colombia, but some of the less closely examined portions of the world nearby.

With Hallowe'en just over a week away, spooky displays have appeared in the neighbourhood. Although we may put out a pumpkin to mark the occasion, we certainly won't need to decorate the garden with spiders and cobwebs. Plenty of those exist here already, which is why I'm waving a "spider stick" in front of me as I head along the shady path. I'd like to find a web with its owner in residence — but not face first.

It doesn't take me long to spot a large filmy structure. It's in perfect condition so the builder must have been up early attending to repairs or reconstruction. I expected to watch her in action, but she's hanging motionless in the centre, upside down, as is her proper posture. Before she began work, she may have made a hearty breakfast out of the old web along with extra helpings of protein from any tiny insects or grains of pollen sticking to it. Spinning an intricate structure like this requires many distinct steps, and it's hard to imagine how a tiny creature manages such a complicated process. We now know she can even learn by experience, adjusting the tension of her strands and upgrading the most successful parts. I watch her for a long time, hoping for some activity: a fly blundering into her trap or the approach of a wannabe mate risking life and limb for his big opportunity. Nothing happens.

Spiders are more patient than I am, so I turn my attention to some chunks of rotting wood lying by the compost bins for no good reason. Under them, I discover a smorgasbord of creepy crawlies, including a couple of centipedes, a tiny flattish snail (normal clockwise spiral and possibly dead), a few red wiggler worms and a number of woodlice.

Woodlice love to lurk under cover of darkness, feeding on decay, so it's no surprise to see them here. However, I don't have long to wait before I notice something unexpected. While most of them scramble to escape from the horrible glare of daylight, two remain rolled in tight balls. I've always assumed that a woodlouse is a woodlouse despite its many common names — sowbug, pill bug, slater, chuggie pig — but maybe I was wrong. I give one a tentative poke. It plays dead, well-protected by the overlapping segments that remind me of miniature armadillos or primordial oceans.

I entice a remaining scrambler onto a leaf for a closer look. A lively fossil, its busy legs carry it with surprising speed onto my thumb, and I promptly shake it off. My less finicky grandson told me he once made dens for woodlice in their backyard, and one of his pets gave birth to pale babies on his hand, miniatures of their mother. Live birth from such a primitive form of life? Obviously, I have much to learn. I replace the chunk of wood gently and return to the house for a hand rinsing and a session online where I discover that sowbugs (the scramblers) and pill bugs (the rollers) are only two of many hundreds of species. And here's news for my grandson — a female woodlouse guards her fertilized eggs in a pouch on her underside. After they hatch, she keeps them on board until they're mature enough to face the world alone. Mother love in marsupial woodlice?

# Red Wigglers

Red wigglers colonized the compost almost as soon as we set up the bins thirty years ago. I've no idea where they came from in the first place, but they've been hard at work there ever since. They consume their own weight in rotting organic material every day and extrude it as pleasant, finely textured soil. In other words, they are perfect recyclers. Which reminds me to mention that neighbour Terry, that other perfect recycler, recently discovered a source of horse manure, two buckets of which she generously passed on to me to add to the compost. The wigglers were no doubt as delighted as I was.

These worms, like earthworms and slugs, are hermaphrodites, and to mate, two consenting adults must line up facing in opposite directions. They exchange sperm in a tricky operation involving slime, and that's it for the fun part. Each worm goes its separate way. The tubular band that forms part of the reproductive system then slides forward to pick up its owner's eggs followed by the donated sperm. After fertilization, the tube slips off to become a cocoon that stays in the ground until the newborns hatch.

One of the wigglers hiding by the compost bins is shorter than the others, and I'm wondering if it met with an accident at some point in its life. It isn't true that a worm cut in half makes two worms, but it *is* true a worm can regenerate a portion of its body, usually the tail end. In the animal world, this isn't a particularly rare ability. Salamanders, sea stars and spiders can regrow an entire replacement limb. Harvestmen, which look like daddy-long-legs, take this whole limb thing to another level. If hunted down by a predator, they can voluntarily shed a leg and leave it as a decoy, twitching independently for up to an hour. Flatworms top the lot with their ability to grow a new head and brain while somehow retaining memory elsewhere in their bodies.

I planned to continue my search for creepy crawlies in the nether regions of the deck, where I hoped to come across a seven-legged harvestman. I pause at the door, however, and discover I've had enough of invertebrates for one day. They've evolved in such weirdly ingenious ways, and their lives are so different from our own that even the most zealous of travellers might find them a touch discombobulating.

# The Importance of Maple Helicopters

I'm standing on the driveway tossing maple seeds into the air, watching them twirl back down like tiny helicopters. They drift sideways to land a fair distance from my feet. It's a perfect demonstration of the tree's strategy to send its progeny out from under its skirts. It's also a childishly simple game that never fails to entertain me.

Unreliable as such clocks may be, I'm still tempted to tell the time of day by blowing on dandelion seed heads. Puff — one o'clock. Puff — two o'clock. Puff — and if the last little parachutes float away, then three o'clock it is! Equally uncertain were the daisy petals I pulled off one by one to discover (no cheating!) if he loved me or

loved me not. Daisy chains were also part of every spring ritual. In summer, we turned snapdragon flowers into talking puppets or held buttercups beneath our chins to prove we really did like butter. We played "shop" with hollyhock seeds for donuts, poppy seed heads for pepper pots and berries for currency. In fall, we battled with conkers, the big horse-chestnut seeds, glossy as polished mahogany, that we pried from their prickly green cases and hung from strings.

Our daughter-in-law told me when she was small in Venezuela, she played "house" by arranging the narrow leaves of bamboo to sketch out rooms and buildings. Indigenous children on this coast make drinking cups from twisted salal leaves, or they play pala-pala by pulling single leaflets from the fronds of sword ferns while holding their breath and saying pala between each one.

I used to assume that youngsters around the world would always enjoy nature's toys, but in 2005, Richard Louv's book *Last Child in the Woods* introduced the term "nature deficit" to describe how children suffered from spending little time in the natural world. Shortly afterwards, the Oxford Junior Dictionary removed many nature-related words in favour of more up-to-date terms such as "blog" and "chatroom" because, as the head of children's dictionaries at the Oxford University Press explained, while many children "used to live in semi-rural environments and saw the seasons," that was no longer the case. Obviously, screen time also played a large part in the change. "Horse chestnut" and "conker" were banished from the dictionary's pages, along with "buttercup" and "dandelion." Even "maple" disappeared. Had children really lost touch with the natural world and with the seasons? Had they lost those early connections with nature that simple pastimes provide?

Thinking back to my own childhood, I wondered how we'd learned to amuse ourselves with nothing more than leaves, seeds and flowers. Had we invented these games ourselves or had we absorbed them from older friends or our parents? I do remember my grandfather showed me how to make a blade of ryegrass squeal by holding it tightly between my thumbs and how, with a penknife, I could fashion a simple whistle from the hollow stem of an elderberry twig. I didn't realize at the time, of course, that ryegrass and elderberry were also becoming part of my vocabulary.

I began to wonder, and worry, about my own grandchildren. Had they spent enough time playing outdoors? Had I helped? Had I pointed out the ring of miniature doves in a columbine flower? (*Columba* is Latin for dove.) Had I shown them how to find the small people who clutch the sides of their bathtubs in Asian bleeding-heart flowers?

At least I must have shown them the rodent lookalikes who tuck their long tails under the foliage of a mouse plant. Its Latin

name is *Arisarum proboscideum*, so maybe I should call it a nose plant? These kids, now grown up, still search them out when they visit the garden.

Things that resemble other things always amuse us. A walk in the woods is far more engaging, for both adults and children, if they know that a Douglas fir cone can be recognized by the backsides of tiny mice that have dived for cover under the scales, that red sorrel tastes like lemon, and that the three-part leaf of a salmonberry minus its top leaflet turns into a butterfly. All this pretending, experimenting and tasting may seem trivial, but it isn't. The maple helicopters of the natural world start us on the path to caring for it.

# Let's Hear It for Damp and Decay!

The latest winds tore branches from the hemlock, littered the deck with fallen leaves and almost obliterated the paths. No surprises there, but I am startled to see that a large patch of glistening red mushrooms has erupted through dark debris in the heart of the jungle. There's something alarming about such an unexpected flaunting of colour. Why are they there?

A large rhododendron grew in shallow soil at this spot until, two summers ago, it succumbed during an unusually dry spell. Two grandsons helped me cut it down. Always on the lookout for shortcuts, I didn't even try to dig out the massive roots. Instead, I covered the short stumps with a thick layer of soil, replanted over the top, added bark mulch and promptly forgot about the whole episode. Now my laziness has arisen from the past to haunt me. Seems I can't get away with anything around here.

These mushrooms provide evidence of decomposition hard at work in the newly soaked mulch, a reminder that much of the garden's activity goes on out of sight. I'm also reminded of an email from my Scottish cousin, who told me about her leaking toilet. The name of her plumbing inspector's company is Damp and Decay, an off-putting but cleverly memorable choice. Although we think of damp and decay as pejoratives, especially in terms of bathrooms, we should be celebrating them. We should be crying out, "All hail the magical moulds and the fabulous fungi!" Our lives, after all, depend on their power to break down and recycle the cast-offs of life.

In this part of the world, Douglas firs and redcedars may grow for 500 years, stand for 500 years and decay on the ground for another 500. In ancient forests, like the one in the park across the road, it's obvious that growth and decay — life and death — go hand in hand. One day, I met a disapproving tourist there. Evidently accustomed to neatly regimented plantations in Europe, he waved his arms in dismay at the chaotic scene. I tried to explain that a genuine old-growth forest is a balance of growth and decay, roughly half and half, where dead wood supports a cascade of biodiversity, from beetles to woodpeckers to bears and just about everything in between. Unconvinced, he departed shaking his head, likely muttering about scruffy Canadians.

After he left, I stood for a moment and tried to see our beloved park through his eyes. Jagged branches jutted from recently fallen giants. Bandy-legged hemlocks straddled nurse logs rotting into mounds of powdery brown duff. Huckleberries sprouted sweetly green from the dark wreckage of ancient stumps. Bracket fungi stepped up standing snags, mushrooms lurked among leaf litter and yellow slime moulds oozed over crumbling logs. Everywhere, life grew out of death. He was right, it was a mess, a bafflingly complicated, glorious mess.

I like to think our backyard jungle welcomes the natural world, but only to a degree. It isn't a nature reserve. Paths and patios must be kept clear, and precious plants rescued from under dumps of tree dandruff. Safety is, of course, a consideration. It's all very well for trees to decay and topple in a forest. Not so much in a garden, albeit a woodsy one. I pause in my survey of the drifted leaf-fall and consider my role in this cyclical world. Immediately, I spot more mushrooms, larger, paler ones with bulging domes. I eye them with respect. I eye the plants around them with a frown. Is all well in their underworld? As head gardener, the little god around here, I'm perched on scales forever trying to keep a balance, deciding how much mess is tolerable, how much decay is healthy and safe. A tough job, that of a deity.

# The Benefits of Boring Journeys

**W**alking, I believe, is good for anything that ails you, and although I'm feeling fine, I'm hoping to bank a little health and wellness. I've made a few circuits of the gravel garden, and now I'm in the jungle making random figures of eight. The paths here twist and turn, intersect and loop back on themselves, inviting a variety of mini hikes.

Charles Darwin at Down House, his home in England, created a circuit on level ground he called his thinking path. It ran beside a meadow and through an unremarkable oak, hazel and holly woodland. He sometimes invited visitors or his children to join him on his daily outing, but usually, he walked alone at a steady pace and, as he described it, in an idle frame of mind. He set out to unwind, probably to escape a rambunctious family life, but most of all, to enter the fluid mental state known as a walker's reverie. I think of it as body boredom. Repetitive physical activities requiring little concentration can help various parts of the brain to mingle easily so that hoarded facts, problems, memories and emotions swill together. In this gently simmering brew, thoughts may coalesce and bubble to the surface in original combinations. And yes, I've had some pretty wild ideas while vacuuming, though none of them constructive.

Scratch a creative brain and you'll likely discover a solitary pedestrian plodding away underneath. Philosophers, poets and writers are famous for it. Virginia Woolf, Robert Frost, William Wordsworth and Wallace Stevens all thought while they walked — and walked and walked and walked — as did Ralph Waldo Emerson and Friedrich Nietzsche. Henry David Thoreau wrote, "Methinks that the moment my legs begin to move, my thoughts begin to flow." Jean-Jacques Rousseau admitted his mind only worked along with his legs. Those tirelessly wagging limbs also liberated the brains of inventors and engineers. James Watt is said to have experienced his eureka moment regarding steam engines while tramping through a park in Glasgow. Inventor Alexander Graham Bell regularly roamed around his Cape Breton home with a favourite walking stick (which visitors can still see at the National Historic Site in Nova Scotia).

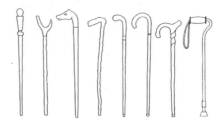

Mozart was another walker, but he also valued carriage rides, and I understand why. Journeys on buses or trains or even behind the wheel can be precious periods of suspension. I think of them as in-between times, the gaps between departure and arrival, when nothing can be done about it. *It* being that low-level, relentless pressure to do stuff. What a guilt trip the Protestant work ethic has laid on all of us who have indeed left undone those things that we ought to have done. No wonder we value a little compulsory downtime, even if it's only in the bathroom. Technology that allows us to be constantly accessible has intruded on the kinds of boring interludes that invite creative brain brews. Would Mozart have composed *The Magic Flute* had he clutched a smartphone?

Recently, I've discovered some new in-between times. With spells of mild insomnia, the small hours have grown familiar, the after-yesterdays and before-tomorrows, the darks before the dawns. I used to fear them, but now I accept them. I keep a pen and scraps of paper at the bedside to jot down any product of the soupy mind that occupies those liberating hours. Sadly, such pearls of perception rarely withstand the scrutiny of daylight. I came across one recently that instructed me to *remember the yellow dog*!

THE BENEFITS OF BORING JOURNEYS 201

Another asserted flatly *beetles are better*. Probably brilliant insights at the time but ones that remain lost to posterity.

Darwin allotted about an hour for his daily walks, the equivalent of ten laps around his thinking path. To keep tabs on time and distance while his mind took itself off among the barnacles, the orchids and the Galápagos Islands, he made a pile of ten stones at the start of each trip and knocked one off with his stick as he passed them by. I'm not as punctilious as Darwin, nor is my time as precious, so I'm not keeping track of my progress on today's expedition. Nor do I expect it to throw any further light on the origin of species, but I am hoping to resolve another of life's enduring mysteries — what's for dinner?

# The Maps We Carry in Our Heads

We all carry maps in our heads, but maps to travellers are like recipes to chefs. So, as a novice travel writer, I've been thinking more deeply about my mental guide to this garden.

Before I began these journeys, my map was little more than a tilted rectangle with features roughed in. A driveway, this shape, at the front. A veggie patch, that wide, at the back. A cedar here, a hemlock there. It told me exactly how to get from the door to the bench by way of the bridge. All very convenient. This year, however, a very different map has been taking shape in my brain, one that's more complicated but also more entertaining.

Every one of my brief outings, whether ten paces or ten laps, ten minutes or an hour, has added fresh information to this new mental map. Here, the sweet scent of a winter flower. There, the gleam of a hummingbird. Here, a baby raccoon. There, a deer with doe eyes and a velvety hide. Chatty chickadees, lacy cobwebs, far too many slugs — such accumulations of notes and images! Across them all, question marks jostle for space.

This layered and lively map pays no heed to boundaries. Memories, like tentacles, reach beyond lot lines, span provinces, cross continents and stretch effortlessly into a past that dates back to my childhood at a school for girls.

One purpose of the educational system at that time was to teach conformity to young women. The intention was to fit us for service as nurses, teachers, secretaries and, of course, housewives. The kinds of jobs in which creativity was not a priority and could even be considered a liability. In our matching uniforms, we plodded through historical dates, irregular French verbs and mathematical equations. We held our tongues and our tennis racquets just so. We made pastry this way, and we sewed on buttons that way. We got it right, or we got it wrong. Passed or failed.

One day, our homework assignment instructed us to map our route to school. Make an original drawing? How thrilling! At last, a task I could tackle wholeheartedly. I spent hours reliving every moment of my daily trip, tracking it with coloured pencils on the largest sheet of paper I could find. In my head, I stepped off the city bus, slogged up the steep cobbled hill, turned under the mysteriously high, ivy-covered wall, scuttled past the beery, possibly dangerous pub and paused at the monumental library where whispering was *de rigueur* and where I'd grown out of Enid

Blyton (hadn't I?) but where the Famous Five adventured on. Past the sweet shop's shiny jars of humbugs and caramels, peppermints and brightly coloured jelly beans. Past the tempting breakfast smells of coffee and pastries wafting from the fashionable new coffee bar, and then a choice between the quick way or the other. Usually the other, where I ducked into the narrow alley and dawdled past the polished brass plaques of ancient law firms or gazed through the dull glass of an antique dealer's window where displays of model boats, tailor's dummies and the faded flags of bygone nations gathered dust.

My lovely map was wrong.

The right map was a small replica of the city's gridded street plan with the route marked on in black ink. The embarrassment! My street corners angled wildly, my main street was ridiculously short, my alley laughably long. And nobody else — nobody! — had marked the pub, let alone drawn multicoloured flags or crayoned ivy (two kinds!) on a wall.

Like that old school map, my new mental vision of this garden is hopelessly out of whack. The asphalt driveway is shorter than the cobblestone path. The turtle pond is as large as its predecessor. A single trillium, ablaze with all the energy of spring, rivals an entire rhododendron. A fern outranks a tree. "Correct" orthographic maps are invaluable, and after spending much of my life working with surveyed site plans, I've grown fond of them. Like history books, however, they can only go so far. They can only tell us what someone else has decided is important. The kind of drawing I made as a child has been called a story map or a memory map.

These kinds of maps may contain as much information as surveys, but it's information of a different order, first-hand and personal. They descend from the earliest human mapping techniques, which must have been verbal and would have been used to record incidents, link landmarks, suggest time frames or point out dangers as well as resources along important routes. Australian Aboriginal songlines are in this tradition, as are Inuit way-finding techniques. Later, these were probably sketched into sand or snow or clay. When such maps eventually became more permanent in the form of pictographs and petroglyphs, they often remained fluid as succeeding generations overlaid their own ideas about what mattered most to them.

My garden expeditions allow me to dig into my mental map for memories and seed it with new stories. Best of all, it has nothing — absolutely nothing — to do with right or wrong.

# Inside and Out

A*ll summer, the garden felt self-contained within the confines of its dense, encircling greenery. I travelled along paths like corridors in a snug and separate world, but now clearings* in the jungle have run together, plump cushions of foliage have deflated, and a robin's nest reveals itself as a dark clot among bare branches. Autumn has exposed the birds' secret places. And mine. Cold winds have unravelled boundaries to reveal the sawtooth skyline of forested mountains. I can no longer pretend this plot of land exists in a place apart. The wider world is getting in.

Of course, in reality my summer garden was never a place

apart. Sparrows, slugs, raccoons and skunks don't give a jot for fences, hedges or lot lines. Neither, unfortunately, do deer (now plural).

All year round, a motley menagerie flutters, clambers, burrows, slithers, scampers, wriggles and simply strolls in and out of this patch of ground we mistakenly call our own. As fall tilts into winter, flocks of migrating birds pass blithely through. The world doesn't just leak in. It pours in. It bombards us with pollen, flies in on the wings of a million insects, and floats in on the gossamer parachutes of dandelions or distant cottonwoods. A thin atmospheric soup of aerosols, dust and chemicals rains down on us as it rains down on Toronto, Cairo or Borneo. The ocean itself creeps in, disguised as salty sea mist. We are cosmopolitan.

It's true that with winter's approach, the garden's defences have frayed. It's true that the wider world is getting in, but here's a thought — maybe I am getting out?

# The Night Shift

Nights come early now, and before we sit for dinner, we close the blinds to shut out the black infinity that seems an affront to our cozy evenings. As suburbanites, we've grown so dependent on electric light that an extended power cut throws us into confusion. We are strangers to the world of darkness.

As a student in the north of England, I worked for a few months on the night shift in a cornflake factory. Wearing a hair net and coverall, I perched on a high stool and dropped promotional trinkets into an endless stream of packets as they wobbled past on a conveyor belt. The Charlie Chaplin movie *Modern Times* recalls the mind-numbing absurdity of the job itself, but my commute by bus to the industrial park was a revelation. As the familiar neighbourhoods faded into sleep, I peered through rain-streaked windows and watched as an unfamiliar townscape emerged. The hooded street lamps punctuated sidewalks with cones of light that cast yellow puddles and turned alleys or empty lots into caves of darkness. The pulse of coloured traffic lights and the sudden swerving glare of headlights so altered the pace and shape of the streets, I felt as lost as if I were travelling through Shanghai or Ouagadougou.

This unfamiliar city was thinly populated by the small stick figures of a Lowry painting. They moved in groups or stood solitary and immobile, silhouetted against the windows of all-night corner shops. Other larger inhabitants occupied the bus itself, and as I huddled inconspicuous in its half-light, I watched their faces reflected in the grimy glass. Pale and drowsy, they seemed utterly withdrawn and self-contained. Only after many hours of dozing through these nightly journeys did I begin to recognize the same people at the same windows and see them as regulars in a sort of shadow society. I felt honoured when they started to accept me as one of their own. At first, a silent nod, but later, a murmured greeting accorded me tentative membership in this mysterious population that rattled nightly through the city.

The parallel world of urban darkness features in many books by travel writer Pico Iyer. In *Video Night in Kathmandu*, he claims that mass tourism threatens ancient ways of life throughout the world and that nighttime is often the last stronghold for authentic cultures and communities. Only in the shadows, he tells us, do their remnants still survive.

It's easy to transfer his thoughts about the impacts of tourism in distant cities to those closer to home in more natural settings. An influx of visitors eager for a taste of the mysterious East in Nepal may not be very different, in effect, from an influx of well-meaning visitors eager for close encounters with whales and grizzly bears on the mystical West Coast of British Columbia.

Across the road in the park, vulnerable creatures have already succumbed to the overwhelming presence of daytime visitors. I can't imagine anyone ever wanted to harm chipmunks and ground-nesting grouse, or encouraged their dogs to do so. Nevertheless, these native creatures have gone. A chipmunk who constantly abandons her meals out of fear is in no condition to breed. A grouse, scared repeatedly from her nest, will eventually lose her chicks. However benign our visits to wild areas may seem, our presence in large numbers threatens a long-established balance. Nighttime is probably the last stronghold for other beleaguered wildlife in the park, as it is for creatures in many parts of the world.

My companions on those late-night buses to and from our shift work in the factories were not part of an ancient way of life, but they were certainly part of a separate group with its own territorial rules and ways of relating to each other. I'm wondering if such communities exist right here in the semi-natural world of our backyards. When daylight belongs to us — the diurnal human "tourists" with our constant fidgeting, our chatter and clatter, our mowers and blowers — does a different cast of characters emerge after sunset? Do whispers of the old, authentic forest come alive then? My daytime journeys have been enlightening. Who knows what I might find if I venture out at night?

# Moonlight

This evening, instead of settling down with my latest haul of travel writers, I'm standing on the deck, gazing up at a gibbous moon. Is it waxing or waning? I'm unsure. How many of us follow its phases nowadays?

Only a century ago, this plot of land was covered with the kind of old growth that still exists in the park. Life there has been forced to adapt to an influx of daytime visitors. I've been wondering if both the forest and the garden slip back at nightfall into some of their ancient moods and habits. Do creatures creep out cautiously into a world of recovered quiet? Do even the trees breathe more easily in rhythms long preceding our hasty human breath?

There's no need to wait for my eyes to grow accustomed to the dark. The deck is awash with pale moonlight and electric light escaping through our kitchen blinds. I make my way down to the gravel garden. There isn't much darkness here either. Vancouver lights fill the eastern sky with a fluorescent glow, and ski hills stain the mountain with splashes of silver. Together, they extinguish the stars and almost outshine the moon itself. I expect to find more darkness in the jungle, but I'm thwarted here again. The neighbouring houses, well camouflaged by foliage through the day, bleed rectangles of brightness into the dusk, and distant buildings on the hillside prick out clearly through the intervening trees. I return to the front garden, where yellow rays from the nearby street lamp filter through cedar boughs and land like spotlights on the wet ground. We are indeed suburban dwellers, firmly on the grid.

I'm reluctant to go back indoors disappointed, so I pause and slowly inhale the chilly air. As usual, patience pays off. I don't see any creatures of the night, but little by little, I notice I'm standing in a garden transformed. Flagstones in the once-upon-a-time pond float like giant lily pads above the gleaming gravel. The ordinary laurel hedge has turned extraordinary, a shimmering brocade. The camellia blinks diamond droplets from the tip of every leaf, and the familiar bamboo improvises unfamiliar, gracefully shifting shadows. I may have failed to find the slightest trace of ancient forest or even true darkness, but I have discovered a surprising beauty. As Margaret Laurence wrote of her time in Somalia in *The Prophet's Camel Bell*, "Sometimes a destination turns out to be quite other than you expected." I'm learning that my destinations *always* turn out to be other than I expected.

# Daring the Dark

I'm not yet ready to give up on my search for traces of ancient, nocturnal life. Eight o'clock was too early, and the moon was too full. A week or so later, I've resigned myself to staying up long after my usual bedtime. I read, watch TV, and to keep myself from nodding off, I get up from time to time to glance outside and check on the neighbouring windows. Is this how owls keep a lookout, waiting for the human lights to flick out one by one?

Eventually, only isolated gleams betray the local workaholics and insomniacs. Time to set out. I switch off the reading lamp and the light in the hallway, but as I pull on a coat and loop a scarf around my neck, I find myself strangely reluctant to leave the house. I will myself to step outside and feel my way down the steps from the deck.

Across the road, the park is a wall of black. The sliver of moon has retreated behind cloud. The city glow has dimmed, and ski hills have shut down for the night. The familiar crunch of gravel hushes as I step onto soft mulch on the jungle path, where I stand still and listen. The faint hum of a distant vehicle trails into the distance, a long diminuendo of the daytime buzz. Then silence — a silence so complete, it rings in my ears.

Stealthy movements overhead are only currents of air creaking through the branches and brushing the hemlock needles. I seem to be alone here. No padding raccoon disturbs the night. No darting vole, no plodding beetle. Sparrows and squirrels are tucked away, dreaming whatever sparrows and squirrels dream, and I've come at the wrong time of year to encounter bats or the restless birds of summer. If a shadow population exists in the garden, it's lying low. An owl, I suppose, could be perched nearby, but those suspiciously bright spots are not eyes, they are bleached hydrangea petals.

Deeper in the jungle, I'm half-blind, and the path begins to lose its way. It's only the firm ground that reassures me. I move forward one step at a time, hands prepared to ward off — what? Faint wafts of damp air? A twig snaps underfoot and shocks like a crackle of lightning. Felty blackness seeps like fog from under the laurels, drifts from shrubby recesses and fingers out from hiding places under the largest ferns. It lurks beneath the bridge. A lair for predators? A sanctuary for prey? My cautious progress begins to feel charged with something feral. Not walking now but prowling, and I'm thinking, is this how it feels to be a cat? Or cougar? I'm no longer sure if I'm seeing or being seen, stalking or being stalked. I hold my breath as if I could shelter in my own warmth, in my own stillness.

I wait.

Sliding from the branches, oozing from the earth, creeping soft-pawed from behind, comes a truly ancient aspect of the world after sundown — a slow, cold shiver of fear.

# Wildlife Theatre

Enough prowling about in the dark. I'm back at the living room window where I can keep an eye on the outside world while I stay warm and dry and conveniently undetected. I often find I'm closer to life in the garden when I'm not actually in the garden.

This morning, I watched a scurry of grey squirrels spiralling around the jungle trees in a thrilling display of agility. This high-velocity hide-and-seek looked like play, but for them, it was serious business. A female would have been the front-runner, leading the males in a madcap race, whirling and streaking from trunk to trunk to test their fitness and their smarts before awarding herself as the prize. These high-energy creatures squeeze two mating seasons into the year and seem undeterred by winter weather.

Eastern grey squirrels, which also come in black, were deliberately introduced to Vancouver's Stanley Park from New York in 1909. Surprisingly, the implant of eight pairs didn't take, and another attempt was made some years later. This time, the population settled in and thrived. I used to wonder how they crossed the First Narrows Inlet, which separates Vancouver from our home on the North Shore. Had these acrobats performed a high-wire act across the Lions Gate Suspension Bridge? I learned the truth a few years back. As the squirrels scampered through the city, some inevitably met with cars or cats, and a wildlife rescue centre accepted the injured. With Stanley Park already overpopulated, a well-meaning helper drove a batch of recovered patients across the bridge and released them in her inviting backyard on our side of the water. Oops!

Now common on the North Shore, they are the monkeys of our jungle, jokers with tails as fluffy as feather boas, who scoot across a road with motions as fluid as cursive script or sit immobile, demure as teapots. Because they have a dubious reputation as harmful invaders and are also avid consumers of tulip bulbs, I feel obliged to disapprove of them. Yet these captivating animals are so patently in love with life, how can I fail to enjoy their presence?

Our native Douglas squirrels are more trustworthy around bird feeders as well as spring bulbs and are always welcome in the garden. If I were to choose a favourite animal, they'd be top of my list, right up there with a favourite tree, the Douglas fir, and a favourite plant hunter, David Douglas. In the early nineteenth century, Douglas, a young Scottish gardener, collected plants and animals in the Pacific Northwest on behalf of the Royal Horticultural Society of London. What he lacked in scientific background he made up for with courage and persistence, and his friendly association with the knowledgeable Indigenous people made him one of the most successful European plant hunters. "I procured some curious kinds of rodents," he wrote of his first encounter with the squirrels that came to bear his name.

# House as a Hide

Once again, I'm enjoying the garden from the living room, where I'm watching a flock of varied thrushes. These are distinguished looking characters with russet waistcoats, smart orange eyebrows and black collars, which they wear like mayoral chains. This afternoon they're visiting our native crabapple tree, and while one or two perch and preen placidly, others perform fluttery gymnastics to snatch the tiny golden fruit from spindly twigs. They are shy birds, but from here, I have a privileged close-up view of their private lives.

Two other red-breasted birds, our local towhees, are gleaning apples knocked off by the busy flock above. A devoted couple, they are tamer than the thrushes and often scuffle in the leaf litter close to me while I'm working. Their fancy footwork reminds me of line dancing. Jump to the front, kick to the back, step to the front, shuffle to the back. I'd love to see them add the Flea Hop or the Mashed Potato to their repertoire.

These living room windows are not the only ones to turn this house into a hide. I've cheered as generations of chickadees have fledged from the nest box outside the studio window. Once, as we ate lunch beside the kitchen window, a great blue heron flapped from the sky, lowered its unwieldy landing gear, and settled on the deck rail a few feet away. Our soup grew cold as we stared in awe at this unexpected visitation from the age of dinosaurs.

And early one morning, from the bedroom window, I caught a sleepy glimpse of something resembling a large black overcoat lying on the path below. I woke up in a hurry when "something" rose and turned into a bear. Before it waddled off down the road, the shameless animal performed unmistakable muscular contractions that left us a large steaming gift.

# Billions and Trillions

The nights now trespass seriously on the days. By five o'clock, the sky is already dusky, and the first faint stars are pricking out. As I stand on the big rock gazing up at them, I recall a saying attributed to science fiction writer Arthur C. Clarke. "Sometimes I think we're alone in the universe, and sometimes I think we're not. In either case, the idea is quite staggering." And suddenly I'm aware — for one awesome and awful moment — that the vastness of space is absolutely real and present. I *know* that I am utterly, nakedly exposed to eternity, that nothing shelters me, not buildings, not trees, not clouds. Nothing.

We hide from such awareness. We bury ourselves in the busy minutiae of our daily lives. We imagine the sky itself is a great protective dome, a perfect hemisphere fitted tightly around the Earth's rim, a dome filled with weathers, awash with golden sunlight or shadowed with silvery moonlight. We've even tried to humanize our nighttime view by joining dotted stars into the familiar shapes of constellations: Great Bear, Orion, Cassiopeia.

How smart I felt as a letter-writing child to add my return address starting with ME at a numbered house on a named street, followed by the town, the country, the continent and then, with a flourish, PLANET EARTH. I ran out of steam at that point, but now I can add the rest of the solar system and the whirlpool we call the Milky Way, made up of hundreds of billions of stars. Hundreds of billions? Can that be right? I'll just add Milky Way Galaxy to my imaginary envelope and move on to the two trillion galaxies (give or take a bunch) rushing, clustered and super clustered through the visible universe that — thanks to stunning photographs emerging from ever more powerful telescopes — becomes more visible by the day.

Trillions? My brain balks at strings of zeros and packs it in around the million mark. I abandon the big rock and retreat to the comfort of the house with its modest street number firmly screwed in place and its lid of recycled rubber shingles securely clamped over my head. The theoretical knowledge, however rudimentary, of where we stand in the scheme of things is not at all the same as experiencing the world as less than a nano-speck of dust leashed to an unremarkable star on the outer edge of forever. Our bone-bound brains can't cope with such a mismatch, and moments of full-on recognition like the one that brushed me briefly this evening are — fortunately? — rare.

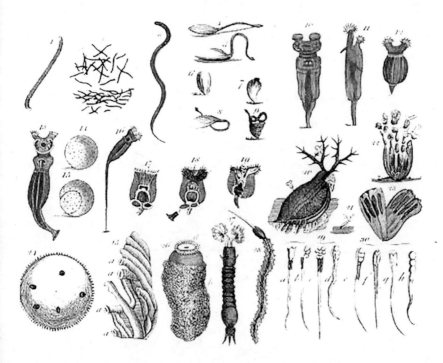

When I set out twelve months ago to explore the world as it exists in this yard, I hadn't thought about the world underground. Nor had I considered the world at night. Tonight, I've come face to face with worlds far beyond my reach of understanding, and I'm forced to think of other worlds that exist on a far, far different scale — those too small for human eyes. It's only thanks to the marvels of microphotography that I'm even vaguely aware of the mites and springtails, the hundreds of nematodes, the thousands of protozoa and millions of bacteria inhabiting every crumb of our compost-rich soil. An astonishing Serengeti. These wonderfully named animalcules swarm through land, sea, air — and us — as lively as tadpoles, enigmatic as ink blots, elaborate as rococo vases, and fanciful as the drawings of a seven-year-old.

I'm not sure where we stand on the spectrum between the incomprehensible world of stars and the fathomless world of bacteria. I feel inadequate to grasp such a stretch in either direction, but as awesome as moments of clarity regarding space may be, I'm inclined to agree with Polish poet and Nobel Prize winner Wislawa Szymborska, who wrote, "I prefer the time of insects to the time of stars."

# The World Nearby

I'm standing on the driveway, holding a small blue flower, thinking about the dark of winter. Few of us enjoy this prolonged period of diminished light, but for many in the past, it must have been more than cold or depressing. It must have been downright scary. What if the sun was ailing or angry? What if it faded out altogether? Around the temperate world, we humans have felt the need to coax the faltering disc back to life with rituals and ceremonies, which not only worked — whoopee! — but brought much-needed warmth and cheer to the dullest time of year.

Scotland is well known for its winter fire festivals, when normally canny citizens take to the streets to swing hefty fireballs, burn tar barrels, or set light to full-sized birch trees soaked in paraffin. If a mob of brawny kilted highlanders awhirl with crackling flames and flying sparks fails to perk up a sickly sun, at least it may help to ward off bouts of seasonal affective disorder. Up Helly Aa in Shetland is perhaps the most famous, though not the most

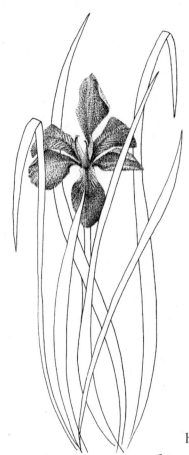

ancient, of such revels. Hundreds of costumed participants, including the all-important Jarl's Squad, elaborately helmeted and kitted out in ways that would have astonished any bona fide Viking, parade through crowded streets at dusk bearing blazing torches, which amid much cheering and lusty singing, they hurl onto a replica longboat. Fuelled by the spectacular inferno and possibly the odd nip of whisky, the festivities continue through the night as citizens live it up in a jolly circus of feasting, drinking, play-acting and dancing.

Our son was born in Shetland at Up Helly Aa. Hours old, he received a ceremonial visit from a splendid Viking troupe, a benediction that probably guaranteed the newborn lifelong immunity to the winter blahs. My immunity isn't entirely foolproof, but as usual, the garden has come to my rescue. Today, when my faith in the future showed signs of wavering, a touch of colour half buried in tufts of grassy foliage caught my eye.

Winter iris grows in parched soil under the eaves of the house, and every year, its fragile flowers reappear in defiance of the gloomy weather. The sky-blue petals of the flower I'm holding are exquisitely marked with tiger stripes and are so insubstantial they barely register under my clumsy fingertips. Here's a promise that, with or without the encouragement of latter-day Vikings, the sun will ride high in the sky once more, and the world will bloom again.

This small treasure speaks to a question that's been on my mind throughout the year. In addition to my many blessings, which include, of course, the garden itself, I've enjoyed the privilege of time. I've had the chance to spend the last twelve months steeped in this world of the nearby. But while I've been reporting on its goings-on, news from the bigger world has been a looming presence, its reports so grave they've threatened to overwhelm such trifling topics as a feisty hummingbird, a motherly woodlouse, or a little blue flower. How can I justify the time spent on such trivia? How to reconcile such disparate aspects of our lives?

After twelve months of mental negotiations, I've reached a settlement. We must pay attention to the big stuff — of course, we must — and act on it as we see fit. The obligation, however, is not the destination. To make our way in peace among such humble gifts as a wren's song, a butterfly, a passing kindness or a smile exchanged, isn't that how most of us would ultimately choose to spend and end our days? And I conclude that this iris, small as it seems, is by no means inconsequential.

I return to my tour of the driveway where the weather may be uninspiring, but the garden is not. On closer inspection, my iris is not the only symbol of hope out here. Below the elm, the unstoppable cycle of seasons is shoving up crocuses and slender spears of daffodils. Newly leafless trees are showing off their secret project of the last few months. Magnolia, dogwood and stewartia have arrayed themselves in brand new buds, some fuzzy, some bunchy, some sleek, but all primed to break out as soon as spring gives the go-ahead. The future is already underway.

I, too, feel eager to get growing, but although we're tilting back to longer days, the bitterest cold is still to come, and our rations of sunshine will be skimpy for some time yet. I should warn the crocuses to slow down. I should warn myself to slow down. Stay tucked underground, pale petals. Stay snug in your dens and your drays, my furry friends. Sleep tight awhile, you garter snakes, you alligator lizards, you little brown bats, all you frail and fluttery things. Be patient all you gardeners, and I'll try to be patient too!

The dimming sky tells me it's time to call it a day, to head back indoors, to place this flower in water, and to hunker down for a cozy evening with a brand-new travel book. It's also time to call it a year. As I look forward to more journeys in the seasons ahead, I hope that you too — in your own nearby — will find many moments of enchantment and peace.

# About the Author

With a career in architecture and landscape architecture, Elspeth Bradbury has also spent much of her life as a writer, a painter and a gardener. She is co-author of *The Real Garden Road Trip*, *The Garden Letters* and the poetry collection *Is That You This is Me*. For more than a decade, she volunteered at VanDusen Botanical Gardens as a Master Gardener and a Garden Guide, taught continuing education classes, and made presentations to garden clubs. She has written and illustrated columns for *The Beacon*, and in 2019, the Ferry Building Gallery presented WILD LIFE, a solo exhibition of her paintings and poetry.